GW00692357

WHAT ARE
THEY DOING
IN THERE?

WHAT ARE THEY DOING IN THERE?

Julia Jeffries
and
Hazel Johnson

QUARTET BOOKS

First published in 2010 by
Quartet Books Limited
A member of the Namara Group
27 Goodge Street, London WIT 2LD

Copyright © Julia Jeffries and Hazel Johnson 2010
Sally Ann Lasson cartoons © Sally Ann Lasson;
Dave Brown cartoons © Dave Brown;
Charles Clarke, Lembit Opik photographs © Getty Images;
Nick Clegg, Theresa's shoes, Jack Straw and Boris Johnson
photographs © Press Association; and
Ill-equipped and Tower of Debt photographs © Hazel Johnson

The right of Julia Jeffries and Hazel Johnson
to be identified as the authors of this work
has been asserted by them in accordance with the
Copyright, Designs and Patents Act, 1988

All rights reserved.
No part of this book may be reproduced in
any form or by any means without prior
written permission from the publisher. Every effort has been
made to seek permission for quotations which have not
been acknowledged in the text. Any omissions are
entirely unintentional and details should
be addressed to the publisher.

A catalogue record for this book
is available from the British Library

ISBN   978 0 7043 7187 3

Typeset by Antony Gray
Printed and bound in Great Britain by
T J International Ltd, Padstow, Cornwall

For Sarah
and the Light Brigade

Contents

Prologue   9

1   *Two Swords and One Foot Apart*   17

2   *Dongle and Twitter*   36

3   *We Have Ways and Means*   56

4   *The Brightest and Best*   73

5   *Wives and Mistresses*   87

6   *Shooting the Messenger*   109

7   *Health and Efficiency*   122

8   *Lost Property*   140

9   *Not Fit for Purpose*   149

10   *Tub Thumping (advice for the next team in to bat)*   164

Bibliography   182

Prologue

Revenge is best served cold . . . in a book
Nora Ephron

It all started with Pamela Harriman. She was a woman who never gave up. As President Clinton once said, 'I am here because she was there.'

Hazel and I also decided 'to come to the aid of the party'. We were tired of being on the outside looking in, constantly wondering *What are they doing in there?* We wanted to do something for our country . . . sounds Kennedy-esque, but there, it was the truth.

Which party we weren't too sure. Obviously not the Labour Party, not after Iraq. We also thought we'd prefer to be on the winning side, although as we sit down to write this book in the months preceding the election, we still can't see who this might be. Right now all three main parties, four if you count the Greens, are jostling for the middle ground. Politics is notoriously cyclical and sometimes there is nothing a party can do, people just want a change of face. Not that whichever party gets in next time will be particularly different. Not in appearance that is. Cameron, Clegg and Miliband have all adopted Tony Blair's mannerisms. Gordon Brown tried this too, but in his case spectacularly un-successfully. It is the way they use their hands (the same parliamentary trainer perhaps?) and the similar suggestion of:

'shucks, you may find this concept too difficult to understand, perhaps moving my body in this particular way will help?' Rather in the way that a certain TV station will have a hit and then all the other stations will copy the format, rather than trying for the more difficult option of coming up with a creative idea of their own.

Ultimately Hazel and I were seduced by David Cameron's 'Vote Blue Go Green' campaign (what happened to that exactly?) and mounted our own speculative campaign for the Conservative Party. We would offer our services as savvy communication experts (Hazel and I have combined experience in advertising, designing and writing), and come to the aid of the Conservatives.

We started off by writing about our speculative campaign to Steve Hilton, Cameron's fixer, but got no reply. We wrote to David Cameron himself, but he asked his PA to put us on to somebody called Anna Marin Ashford who did not especially want to see us . . . in fact she refused to take calls and ignored our e-mails. It started to seem that a great deal of time is spent on the greasy pole pushing people off.

Then we 'crossed the floor' and wrote to Vince Cable who referred us on. No response. Then Caroline Lucas. No reply of any kind. Although our visual campaign dealt with very important issues like red-tape, poorly equipped soldiers, global warming, the credit-crunch (and take note, our campaign began several months before the FINAL COLLAPSE . . . we were clairvoyant too), the strange thing was not one of the parties was interested in our cut-price brilliance. Our message was 'throw away all those advisers that cost you a fortune. We are twice as good and half the price.' This was our pitch, but nobody could care less about saving money. Funny. But this was then. Now is now.

ILL-EQUIPPED

UNDER LABOUR

Not ones to give up (think Pamela Harriman), we found a way in to see Theresa May, who gave us the kind of welcome more usually associated with walking into a deep freeze. Of course our first glance was towards her feet . . . unremarkable that day . . .

but she was wearing a strange diaphanous blouse with a ruffle that made her look like a cross between Charles I and Madame Arcati. Our whole campaign had a lot of Noël Coward about it at this stage so the image came to mind. She gave us quite a grilling but we held up surprisingly well. Politically Hazel and I know our stuff, and it helped our cause that Hazel has worked in advertising while I can field a verbal punch.

We launched into why we'd be interested in helping her with 'Women to Win', which happened to be a campaign she was fronting. She looked puzzled and said she had enough women on her team. This was only a few months before Cameron, apparently despairing about the quality of his candidates, asked for men and women from all walks of life to put themselves forward. Perhaps this was merely a sham proposition anyway, since a man who responded in good faith to this clarion call wrote to the *Telegraph* complaining that Cameron hadn't even deigned to reply to his seemingly credible application. Enough men perhaps? None of it really stacked up . . .

Anyway Theresa was keen to be shot of us so we were sent to 'Branding'. All roads lead to here. It reminded me of a poem by James Reeves called 'Leaving Town': *It was impossible to leave the town/bumping across a maze of obsolete rails/three times we reached the gasworks and reversed.*

'Branding' is a buzz word (and also a complete department, not that we ever got there so we can't personally testify) that has been around since spin began and is not to be confused with the now controversial issue of hot irons on the flanks of Shetland ponies. Still, whichever way you looked at it we were getting nowhere.

Indefatigable (Pamela again) we also wrote to Boris Johnson who (obviously) passed us down the line. We were sent reams of forms to fill in, the subtext being 'don't bother us . . . We are an equal-opportunities employer but this doesn't mean you.' Later Boris was seen jumping about describing small businesses as the backbone of London, although Hazel and I discovered that his own 'competitive procurement procedures' involved visiting websites requiring data which would take days (or years) to fill in, a task too time-consuming for any but the largest company. We then sent him a reproving letter ourselves and a copy of Lucy Kellaway's *Who Stole My Blackberry* because it seemed so apt. One of his people did thank us for the book. A response of a kind.

Ann Widdecombe came up trumps though (dear Ann) and sent us a lovely letter saying how much she liked looking at 'our samples' and promised to pass them on . . . yes, unfortunately to 'Branding'.

As our final salvo we even made a film called 'Cameron's Cat', filmed on the roof of my house (our own version of *Touching the Void*), to show David Cameron to what lengths we would go to get a good shot. We got an insider to put our film on Cameron's desk, but like so much lost government data it is presumably languishing at the bottom of somebody's pile, unloved and unwatched (anyone interested can see it, though, on YouTube or www.foxandangel.com).

Still, having now actually penetrated the building where it all happens and viewed Theresa May's shoes in person, we were thoroughly intrigued. There seemed to be a lot of activity, but we wondered how much of it was of use to anyone, particularly constituents. 'Constituents' are still 'constituents' but it can only be a matter of time before the House of Commons finally falls on its own sword and they are restyled 'customers'. MPs attest to being 'very busy people' and a number of them have used this lame excuse to justify 'oversights' re their expense claims. But we wanted to know what they were actually busy at. It was reading Chris Mullin's diary during the course of our researches that gave the lie to the assumption that MPs do a lot of important work. 'I resolutely refuse to waste time ploughing through piles of paper-work to no effect whatever.'

Diaries by Ferdinand Mount (Thatcher) and Bernard Donoughue (Wilson) made us even more suspicious.

It was very difficult to gain any access to Parliament. What with vetting and frisking it was made pretty clear you were in a very secure area, suggesting that MPs themselves do not hold their constituents in particularly high regard. In fact we were very shocked to discover how condescending MPs were towards their electorate. 'I don't think your average Jo Bloggs would be interested in that/is clever enough to see that,' etc., etc. All those educational targets and social improvements didn't seem to have actually filtered down to the electorate, not as far as MPs are concerned at least. An MP quoted by Chris Mullin said, 'No good trying to appeal to everyone. About 60% of the electorate will do.'

Samantha Cameron has recently gone on record as saying she 'knows nothing about politics like most people and it means nothing to her', which is a disingenuous statement if ever there was one; clearly implying that politics must be left to those 'in the know', as understanding it is very difficult and we musn't fret our pretty dim heads about it, while also trying to say that she wasn't about to meddle in Dave's politics herself . . . which may or may not be something we find reassuring.

In fact it is an indictment of society that we know so little about how we are run and ruled. When Edward Heath posed this dangerous question with the intention of bringing the nation to heel, the voters would have none of it and turned him straight

out of office. It is that old, old cliché but 'the personal is the political'. Where we shop, every letter we (used to) post, every train we catch, every NHS appointment – everything is a political act about which we surely need reminding. And we'd better wise up to it soon or, as Johann Hari has observed in the *Independent*, 'If you don't turn on to politics, politics will turn on you. In any society the people who already have power will try to get the state to work in their interest.'

The funny thing was that David Cameron, in his speech to Conference, talked about everything Hazel and I had included in our (by now on-line) campaign. Spooky or what? Was it a case of 'talent borrows' or 'genius steals'?

The more we researched this book the more we discovered that everything in politics had a natural cycle which seemed immutable. A new administration started off bright-eyed and bushy-tailed only to be brought down by one scandal after another, ending in ignominy and bluster.

The Victorian novelist Anthony Trollope wrote: 'Power is so pleasant that men quickly learn to be greedy in the enjoyment of it, and to flatter themselves that patriotism requires them to be imperious.'

It is presumably because of this human failing that American Presidents are limited to two terms.

And furthermore, as Trollope says: ' . . . and in the battle of politics, as it goes, men are led further and further away from first causes, till at last a measure is opposed by one simply because it is advocated by another, and members of Parliament swarm into lobbies, following the dictation of their leaders, and not their own individual judgements.'

Where was the moral authority in all this?

The Conservative Party may not have taken our speculative campaign on board, but by now we were on the case with the bit between our teeth. So, like Pamela Harriman, here we go: *What are they doing in there?* Let the story unfold . . .

1

Two Swords and One Foot Apart

It is only when the threat of popular participation is
overcome that democratic forms can be safely contemplated.

Noam Chomsky

Old Father Thames keeps rolling along . . . there can surely be
no better place for a palace than on this great London river.
Edward the Confessor knew what he was doing building upon
such a splendid vantage point. This is where we started our
investigation, with a visit to the Houses of Parliament. The
public can do so during the summer recess and it only took a bit
of hard work navigating the website to get hold of some tickets.
The visit turned out to be both more and less revelatory than we
supposed.

The tour starts in Westminster Hall, first built in 1099. It has a
magnificent carved angel roof, (reminding us of Tony Blair's
Messiah period, when he was little lower than the angels) and
this is where medieval and Tudor tub-thumping took place. It is
a vast awe-inspiring building which has survived fire, flood and
pestilence (swine flu and so on). You cannot fail to be reminded
of history and heritage. It is magnificent, empty and still. This is
where you assemble – twenty minutes early are the instructions,
don't even think about being late – to meet your leader.

No, not Gordon Brown, even he can't be everywhere, but your guide for the next hour and a half. The tour takes place at a brisk pace, but as the palace is on an eight acre site it's merciful that you don't see it all. The first 'Dear Bill' letter in *Private Eye*, purporting to be from Denis Thatcher, described the place as 'just an antiquated rabbit warren – miles and miles of corridors'. It helps to pick up a guide book, which isn't a definitive history but useful all the same. It has a worthwhile map, pointing out the toilets and the shop, and contains photographs of MPs doing all kinds of interesting things. It is not too highbrow, this would never do, and in fact it is something of a mood piece. It seems to be there primarily to reassure: 'Parliament and government each play a part in forming the laws of the United Kingdom. They are separate institutions that work closely together, so it's easy to mix up what each one is responsible for!'

Well, OK then . . . we mustn't feel bad if we can't absorb everything straight away. Not that you will have time to read it en route; instructions for the march are made clear from the very beginning. 'No drugs, alcohol or photography' (although we were photographed at the start and had to wear our mug-shots round our necks), and 'I have to keep you all in my line of vision' (so no idling, keep up). These rules had to be shouted out to us as several tours begin simultaneously and the vast space echoes.

The Houses of Parliament adjoining the medieval hall were designed by Charles Barry, who was the winning architect out of ninety-seven entries. Then the designer A. W. N. Pugin added the furniture and fittings. They were a brilliant and inspired pairing. Both within and without this building, in twenty-first-century lingo, is quite definitely 'fit for purpose'. Its magnificent clock-tower (Big Ben) chimes for England and represents all that is serious and proper. (Although apparently this symbolism is supposed to be phased out shortly from news programmes for being too 'London-centric', which makes no sense, in fact is completely barmy.)

Unlike Britain's unloved towns and tawdry shopping malls, the Houses of Parliament are expertly maintained and something to which the country can aspire in the absence of inspiring leaders. Thank goodness it still stands proud (please to remember the fifth of November, gunpowder, treason and plot). There are no two ways about it, this is a truly wonderful building and anyone who can visit should do so.

We were fed various factoids such as: for the State Opening of Parliament the Queen wears her 'best hat' (tour-speak for crown), which is fetched from the Tower of London. As each session begins the monarch outlines the legislation which will be attempted. 'Attempted' being the operative word in the case of the current government. With only a few months till the election they can propose whatever legislation they like without the responsibility of actually having to carry it out.

At present there is a running battle about ceremonial dress. The new Commons Speaker has refused to wear his in the name of modernity, but we agree with Francis Young, writing in the *Telegraph* that 'Ceremonial dress exists to assert the truth, important in a constitutional monarchy, that the office matters more than the person'. In light of recent scandals this seems more vital than ever. This is the same reason that judges wear wigs; it should serve to remind them and others of the gravity and importance of their position.

But . . . on with the tour . . . unwanted facts were dished out thick and fast and we digressed slightly to look at a painting of Henry VIII, but were immediately rebuked by our leader. *'There is always one,'* we could see her thinking. This tour is whistle-stop and not for anyone interested in painting, or even architecture. Fortunately, however, the architecture is so in your face you couldn't possibly miss it. In one of the main lobbies there are some larger than life bronze statues of previous Prime Ministers. Churchill's is outstanding; he was such a distinctive character and it captures his essence, but the one of Mrs Thatcher is disappointingly coarse and rather androgynous. We were rushed through so can't remember if she was holding her famous handbag.

The momentum of the tour couldn't distract from the gravitas and beauty of our surroundings. At the risk of repeating ourselves it is a truly remarkable building and there cannot be a greater honour than having the good fortune to gain a seat here as a Member of Parliament.

Not that we rag-bag of lesser mortals were allowed to sit. There were a couple of pit-stops where we could rest, but in the House of Commons itself we had to stand and shuffle or perch awkwardly on steps. The hallowed seats themselves were *verboten*. We couldn't make out if this was a moral issue or because we might wear out the leather. Would visitors reach under the seats to plant bugs, secret cameras or bombs? Anyway it was a pettifogging diktat and awkward for anyone with a stick or minor disability . . . not to mention quite irritating when you consider how the current administration has puffed itself up about equal access issues.

The two red lines that run the length of the chamber are called Sword Lines. Once upon a time when Parliamentarians carried swords there was danger of fights developing between the two sides and these lines were instigated as a measure against this threat. They are two swords, and one foot apart. Any MP who speaks must do so from behind these lines. This is where the expression 'to toe the line' is thought to originate.

'Crossing the floor' is what it is called when one MP defects to another party, which seems completely undemocratic and we are very surprised that it is even allowed. Paul Marsden, one-time MP for Shrewsbury and Atcham, defected from Labour to the Liberal Democrats in 2001 over the war in Afghanistan. Bizarrely, this bed-hopping MP (exposed as a love-cheat) floor-crossed back to Labour in 2005. More recently Quentin Davies moved from Tory to Labour. And of course there was the great floor crossing in the 1980s when the Social Democratic Party set itself up; off marched Roy Jenkins, Shirley Williams, David Owen and Bill Rogers with their swords.

Defecting is a risky business (Marsden has a sword decorating his wall at home just in case) and the SDP vanished later to be merged with the Liberals to create a new party, the Liberal Democrats. Feeling honour bound to resign over an important issue is fair enough but it seems arrogant to think you can be an MP for one party when you were elected as part of another. Surely a by-election should be called and the electorate should declare your fate? Like a board game – you should miss a turn and go back to the start, hoping that your new party will take you on as a candidate somewhere else, although why they would want to we have no idea. How can the electorate be sure it was a genuine crisis of conscience? Might it not be a case of seeing which way the wind was blowing and jumping ship before the boat sank?

A similar situation can arise during a coalition government, as Anthony Trollope saw only too well: 'It was quite understood that Sir Timothy was inimical to the Coalition though he still belonged to it, and that he would assist in breaking it up if only there were a fair chance of his belonging to the party which would remain in power.'

This could be very relevant in 2010 if no party achieves an all out majority.

Other useful information gleaned on tour was that Prime Minister's Questions is on a Wednesday from 12.00–12.30 pm and that for this you have to obtain tickets. We later discovered this was not at all easy. We had a huge struggle, almost as if we were trying to get hold of state secrets. Pamela Harriman would never have put up with it. We tried a number of different routes but this was typical of the response: 'I don't want to be unhelpful but who passed you on to us? We are in discussion with them about how many tickets we can give out . . . we are still in negotiation. Let me get back to you.' They never did. Fortunately our local MP Charles Hendry came up trumps with tickets. He also agreed to be interviewed which was very brave and sporting.

We were there the day of the pre-budget speech so there was excitement and expectancy in the air as well as a full house. As Anthony Trollope wrote: 'A personal quarrel [which is very much what PMQs tends to be] is attractive everywhere. The expectation of such an occurrence will bring together the whole House of Commons.' From above the Commons still looks ornery and Pickwickian in character, packed with large tummochs (a cross between a tummy and a stomach), and flushed faces. Peter Hain was there with a very out of season sun tan. Is he aware of government warnings about sun-beds . . . or do you go this strange orange colour if you forget to declare donations to your leadership campaign? Perhaps this heightened colour is just another version of Pinocchio's nose.

There are microphones everywhere, although one MP, I think it might have been Quentin Davies, couldn't seem to hear and was having to cup his ear. There was a lot of back-chat as well; conversations going on everywhere, nothing to do with the lesson, and John Bercow had to shut them all up like an old-fashioned headmaster. He was surprisingly good at this and in the end Nick Clegg ('Mr Clegg must be heard') was allowed to voice his rejoinder.

Nick Clegg

There was also the usual guff of course: 'the spending environment', talk of a 'deficit reduction plan' (joke), and 'more police on the streets' (that again) and special allowances arranged for people who like bingo and/or had an old boiler.

Women's voices were lost in the general hubbub; the acoustics certainly seem to favour the baritone. The women didn't help themselves by sounding rushed and apologetic and in any case few were hit upon by John Bercow in spite of the fact that they were jumping up and down as if they were in an aerobics class. The leaping was led by Hazel Blears and her two accomplices although in the end only Hazel got to speak. The men got up and down in a different way, more as if they were trying to avoid Deep Vein Thrombosis, which by the look of them was quite likely.

Gordon Brown appeared beleaguered and embattled throughout. He is trying to do too much you might say, especially as he was off to Afghanistan in full defensive regalia, including stab vest and helmet (no obvious shortage of equipment then), the next week. Although I suppose he might have thought, 'It will be good to get away'. Couple MPs didn't seem to sit next to each other and not all the wives could be seen. Perhaps there was a bit of 'you go darling, the budget's more your thing. I'll go and get the Christmas tree. Tell me if anything interesting crops up'. Or there might be, 'Your turn, I looked in last week, bound to be a bore'.

Alistair Darling droned on and on but his personality seemed ideal for the occasion. He was inscrutable, but with the country owing billions and trillions of pounds (the man in the street just lost count) and its soul ransomed to the bankers, this was obviously the only way. Cameron and Osborne sounded clear and clever on this particular day; they have that diction associated with modern Eton, no longer plummy or over cultivated, but sharp and easy on the ear.

You can't in fact hear what is going on from the public gallery as well as in the old days because of the blast proof screen. Still, it's obviously needed. The day we were at PMQs a man stood up and went 'WOOOOO' and had to be strong-armed out.

The Parliament brochure showed a photograph of a full house, but also explained why it was usually pretty empty. We noticed that a lot of the Labour side rushed out to lunch once their man had spoken, which looked pretty damn rude to the other side. And it thinned even more when Vince Cable started up. Obviously no one wanted to hear good sense. We suppose MPs also had other things to do, committees and so on.

The average length of a daily sitting is just over 8 hours although not much of that is actually spent in the chamber and of course

MPs need breaks. There were toilet signs everywhere but heaven knows what would have happened if somebody answered a call of nature on our official tour. You would move out of range and therefore probably be machine-gunned. The day we were there the place was full (even apart from tour parties, which made it even fuller) with a spattering of pretty researchers carrying clipboards and a lot of armed guards mooching about looking for action without finding any.

We found out that on some tours you are allowed to venture 'off-piste' to look at paintings as and when you like. But as we were to discover from the expenses and other scandals, this is a place where rules are often interpreted differently, for we weren't.

The Central Lobby is 'the heart of democracy' where you can exercise your right to lobby, 'the end of a long journey from one king one vote to one person'. Apparently when a member of the public makes a request to lobby an MP, the doorkeeper will be sent to look for him. Is it as simple as that? It wasn't simple for 100 cub scouts who wanted to lobby recently; they were too young. Surely you would be frisked and need your photograph taken at the very least, but the guidebook suggests not. Lobbying is a grey area shrouded in secrecy. It must go on . . . companies and corporations are known to lobby, especially in relation to armaments, drink and tobacco, but how, when and why was impossible to find out. To lobby is a bit like procuring – it has shades of meaning (think Christine Keeler).

The House of Lords is as grand as the Commons, in fact more so, although in need of further reform. It has long been a neat way to hasten the exit from the commons of unsatisfactory MPs, always a useful sweetener. At the moment it is neither aristocracy nor democracy, but since no one has any idea how to improve the problem, they have decided 'it is not a priority'. Getting rid of the hereditaries was the political expedient, but what to do next was a blank. John Major thought that an elected upper chamber would result in stasis and nothing but rivalry between above and below. Right now it is not at all satisfactory, but nobody knows how to sort it.

We happened to hear a junior shadow minister (junior doesn't mean younger in the Parliamentary sense, another confusion, even though it conjures an image of short trousers) speak recently who rashly said the Tories were preparing for government and as soon as they got in they would have to make more Lords, otherwise they'd never get their legislation through.

There was no mention of freshly parachuted-in Labour Lords like Digby Jones, Sugar and Mandelson being possibly parachuted out again to even things up. Those who were sceptical about Alan Sugar fitting in should know his maiden speech reiterated his 'honest man/humble origins/great wealth' credentials in case we should fail to 'get it' (why he was there and so on). In other words demonstrating that he is just as capable of putting people down as any other Lord.

The latest 'big idea' to allow life peers to resign and be elected to the Commons would lead to more jumping between the houses, although what could be the advantage in this for the electorate? It might be counter-intuitive, or plain wrong, but are the Lords and Ladies we have now actually more effective and representative than the old system? How about a jury system to select some noble lords? Or a lottery – there would just be time for one before the election. What could be fairer and more original? New Labour loves a lottery! Why not combine the two systems. Anyone who was 'called' would have to sit for a certain amount of time, a bit like jurors, and then simply be moved out to make way for the next incumbents. There are a lot of musical chairs anyway, Black Rod would cope, and it seems the obvious solution.

The best idea for the Lords came from Miland Joshi in a letter to *The Times*: 'If a reformed upper house is to embody wide experience in human affairs with a detachment from party politics in favour of the national interest, it should be nonpartisan. Therefore to qualify for election to it, candidates should have to take an oath not to join, serve or accept favours from any political party, and renounce any association that exists before they stand.'

Apart from the phrase 'regime change' which is banned, and 'climate change' which is contested, there is one word that both Houses are fond of: it is 'change'. Left or right they all love it and all treat it as if it were a newly minted word. Lord Falconer admitted that 'people are fed up with the Government' . . . (that slow dawn) and said forthrightly, 'We need to make changes'. David Cameron's latest leaflet to drop through our door says, 'Vote for Change', 'It's time for Change', 'Changing in Europe' and 'Plan for Change'.

'Change' was once also a euphemism for a 'cut', but now cuts are good they can be called 'cuts'. All parties are competing to cut the most, and the more swashbuckling and wide-ranging these cuts are the better. So 'change' has turned into 'choice' and 'choice' is more than just an idea . . . it seems to be thought that if you repeat it often enough it will morph from sound bite into actual policy. The next election will, according to Gordon Brown, be of the 'big choice' kind.

Anthony Trollope could see through this kind of spin (it was called propaganda in his day) and was a stickler for propriety: 'A Man who entertains in his mind any political doctrine except as a means of improving the conditions of his fellows, I regard as a political intriguer; a charlatan and a conjurer . . . as one who thinks that by a certain amount of wire pulling, he may raise himself in the estimation of the world.'

Neither was he blind to the reality that then, as now, becoming an MP could be financially advantageous. It's amazing how little has actually 'changed' between then and now. Trollope was rightly sceptical about the merits of having MPs on boards of companies just because they are MPs. He hit the nail on the head some hundred and fifty years ago about directorships: 'People are still such asses that they trust a Board of Directors made up of members of Parliament, and therefore of course members are made welcome.'

In fact researchers at Harvard have discovered that the financial benefits that accrue from just winning a seat are considerable. The study concluded that earnings of successful MPs are twice that of candidates that ran unsuccessfully. Becoming an MP still confers status and grandeur as it should, but also access to board rooms and other unelected bodies from which extra income can be derived. MP Nick Raynsford (Labour) for example earned £148,000 for six public sector jobs last year and John Hemming (Lib Dem) took a salary of £200,000 from his own software company, although it was discovered that Tory MPs profited in this way the most.

The report had a useful corollary which declared that American politicians were paid twice as much as their English counterparts and noted that Members of Congress haven't been able to take on paid directorships since the 1970s . . . the argument that directorships confer public benefit has always been a specious argument but one much guarded by MPs because they say it contributes to their understanding of what is going on outside Parliament.

If being an MP is so part-time why not introduce job-share,

one of them in town and one in the constituency, although we suppose that would induce squabbling. You don't hear of nurses and dustbin men (sorry, amenity support officers), being paid a full salary for half a week, why not housewife MPs, teacher MPs, plumber MPS, fashion editor MPs . . . or MP social workers and carers for the elderly MPs? Ann Keen started as a nurse MP and remained registered, so she must have done some part-time nursing at least. How about BT engineer MPs, call-centre MPs? There could also be scope for ex-con MPs – Jonathan Aitken could be recalled from the wilderness, or even Lord Archer.

If their directorships are so part-time why are they so lucrative? This is something that needs to be looked at and is an issue that all parties have shied away from. Boris Johnson was reported to describe the £250,000 a year he earned from journalism as 'chicken feed' and was rightly ridiculed. All this should be factored in (and out) when the expenses saga is mulled over and the issue of MPs salaries and other earnings are examined. Anyone who doesn't take all these factors into account is ducking a central issue. Ducking has become a tricky word too, a bit like 'procurement'.

It has occurred to us that there is surprisingly little actual debate these days. MPs don't even have to show up in the debating chamber now they have monitors in their offices; they can veto anything that looks boring, and obviously they do. Prime Minister's Questions is about point scoring and acting out certain roles. Since Gordon Brown has been at the helm there have been a lot of temper tantrums and signs of strain. What a contrast to Tony Blair who even when sending the country to war remained calm, slightly apologetic it has to be said, but unruffled. Nothing is actually furthered in these debates; it is a piece of theatre, a bit of push and shove and that is as far as it goes.

Still at least MPs show up in the chamber on Wednesdays. A researcher who works for a junior shadow minister described to us his boss's day. On the day described the MP seemed very busy, but his schedule did not include a visit to the chamber at all. Some MPs avoid it whenever possible. MP Bill Deedes thought that trying to become a Commons star was 'a fool's errand'. Bill's opinion was that speaking in the Commons, with all the anxious preparation that was required if you wanted to make a mark, was not an efficient use of time or a good way of getting noticed. And getting noticed was obviously what it was all about.

Many famous politicians have needed a lot of help with their delivery: David Lloyd George was once drafted in to show Harold Macmillan 'how to use his upper body and particularly the full length of his arms when making a point and not just to flap about'. According to Charles Williams, Macmillan's biographer, in the early days he was once thought 'more like a wet fish than a man'. He was also 'considered hopelessly boring, always button-holing people to lecture them on some subject that they were not in the least interested in'.

Not that being boring stopped him standing for office and he made such great improvement in his delivery that he was Prime Minister from 1957–1963. (If at first you don't succeed . . .)

As has often been said: 'decisions are always taken *somewhere else*'. Everything seems to happen in distant offices, rather like in Michael Frayn's play *Noises Off* when the stage itself remains empty and the audience is left to guess what is going on from the actors' brief appearances and dialogue spoken from the wings.

In the 1990s, not really so very long ago, this 'somewhere else' was the Savoy Grill. As *The Sunday Times* reported: 'Through these doors, every weekday lunchtime, pass cabinet ministers and multi-millionaires, politicians and peers, newspaper editors and bankers; the entire pin-striped fraternity of the power lunch persuasion.' These meetings were, it goes without saying, for men. It was ever thus, certainly as far back as the nineteenth century as witnessed by Anthony Trollope: 'He [the PM] understood clearly that though they were gathered together at Gatherum Castle [aka Chequers, perhaps, or maybe a yacht in the Med. or a banker's rural estate], for festive purposes, yet that no time was unfit for the discussion of State matters. Does not all the world know that when in autumn the Bismarks of the world [Mandelson, say], or they who are bigger than Bismarks, meet at this or that delicious haunt of salubrity, the affairs of the world are then settled in little conclaves, with greater ease, rapidity and certainty than in large parliaments or the dull chambers of public offices?'

However history will judge Tony Blair, he changed things for women without a doubt. 'Blair's Babes' had their difficulties but he turned the women's vote to his advantage, divining that women were now ready to vote for other women, when in the past they had colluded in the status quo and, with exceptions, remained happy for their leaders to be men. This idea lurched into reverse thrust when he gave a speech to the Women's Institute in 2000, and discovered that the women's vote cannot be taken for granted. They did not adore him quite as much as he thought and tried to boo him off stage. David Cameron knows he will not win next time round if he cannot get more women on board; it is one of his many pressing challenges.

This being said, Lesley Garner writing in the *Daily Telegraph* in 1992, says this about women: 'To survive in Parliament, women must behave like men. They must keep men's hours [changed, but many say not for the better], stand up and shout like men and generally take enough heat to justify their place in the kitchen. No wonder they end up hard-boiled.' If you read this in the *Telegraph* in 2010 you still wouldn't blink.

MPs, since the expenses scandal, have all retreated behind closed doors. The penalties for going off message or being even mildly politically incorrect could cost them their job now. In Parliament the enemies within are just as menacing as a disillusioned electorate. Despite all the anti-bullying and equality/diversity medicine that the government dispenses for the likes of the rest of us, bullying is known to be as rife as bloody-mindedness in Parliament, but defended as the normal thrust and parry of good office.

Gordon Brown is thought to be a bully but also a ditherer. The same junior opposition minister who let it out that the Tories were 'preparing for government' also said everyone in the Labour Party wanted him to go and hoped his wife Sarah would 'say something'. This clairvoyant also predicted Gordon would be 'gone in months' while in fact he is still there and Sarah, far from having a quiet word, has upped her public appearances and before Christmas appeared in the newspapers showing off her collection of knitted woollen hats.

At least she is supporting him. Marcia Falkender, Harold Wilson's fixer and sort of wife substitute (Mary, his actual wife, wisely kept out of the way), terrified him and got in a stew when he employed a new PA. Bernard Donoughue was working for Wilson at the time. This is an extract from his diary: 'Marcia arrived at Chequers unexpectedly yesterday and found Janet working there. Things are warming up on that front. The PM knows it and looks worried – he retreated to the flat before lunch and sent for Joe to come and see him there. This was so Marcia could not find him in his study. He also left by the front lifts and out through the front door so as not to pass Marcia's room.'

Right now is not a good time for MPs to be putting their heads above the parapet. It is an irony that most of the parapets and terraces are currently out of bounds for health and safety reasons. In fact the only person to get up that high, apart from members of the Health & Safety Executive, presumably, is Emma Gibson who recently scaled the Houses of Parliament and spent 28 hours sitting on the roof (followed by 24 hours in a cell in Charing Cross police station). MPs and their families are still allowed to use the Crypt Chapel for weddings, and also shortly for civil partnership ceremonies. It may even be available soon for use by the general public. Although presumably this would stop it being a perk.

And there is always the division bell to consider. When the bell goes the whips expect MPs to drop everything and get themselves in through the division lobbies. What happened to Cyril Smith, the very large and stalwart member of the old Liberal Party, we wonder? How did he get through? It's not that wide a gap. Was he squeezed through by a team of pushers? We hope it wasn't the scene of his fatal demise. There is an underground tunnel between Portcullis House and Westminster (it is quite a hike) and you can see whipped-in MPs belting through from one place to another to cast their votes.

Not much need for whipping-in right now however; it seems as if they have all become like Lord Fawn, Trollope's timid junior minister who always follows the party line and is perpetually anxious about offending his superiors. Or in this case, journalists writing for the *Daily Telegraph.* Since the expenses crisis apparently MPs feel neutered and emasculated . . . victims in fact. Will there soon be an appointment of a Tsar? Not for all; some are refusing to pay back the money and are mounting a rearguard action.

Fortunately it has never been a British characteristic to show undue deference to politicians or Prime Ministers. We have been

astounded to hear American Presidents deliver the most inane statements ('war on terror', 'axis of evil' and so on) which they appear to think profound, or at least very carefully considered, and deliver in a frighteningly serious and thoughtful way. These pronouncements seem to be swallowed whole by the mute and choreographed media. There is no chance of jumping up with a tricky question and putting Presidents on the spot, everything is controlled and reverential.

Anthony Sampson in his memoir *The Anatomist* remarks how little respect is shown in Britain towards the elected leader whilst in America 'Nixon could call on his friends to ask sympathetic questions while his enemies were silenced'.

Sampson was right that we 'are lucky to have a monarchy which separates the pomp from the politicians', but we wonder how worth the candle all this free speech in the free world is, when much of it is so banal, so over-simplified so that we can all, especially those who think we are 'worth it', 'understand'.

It is just as well the British people are suspicious of posturing, creationism and anything happy-clappy. We will tolerate most things except leylandii. Chris Mullin was overjoyed to report that: 'No 10 are saying they will not, after all, stand in the way of our attempt to legislate on high hedges, providing we don't seek a slot in the government's programme. The plan is to draw up a bill which we will offer to someone who comes high in the ballot for private members' bills. I have asked if I, rather than Michael Meacher, can make the announcement in the hope of being permitted a tiny footprint in the sand as a result of my otherwise fruitless year in office.'

2

Dongle and Twitter

House of Commons Department of Resources: 'Deputy Trans-actional Manager'. You will manage two administrators and provide support for the Commercial Services Directorate assisting the Procurement Managers with their Contract/projects. Im-plementing a new e-procurement tool you will be required to be fully conversant with its operation and able to train others as necessary. Experience of dealing with professional budget holders and other colleagues to obtain information at key project stages from various resources is desirable.

Job advert, July 2009

We feel absolutely sure that when Bill Gates turns on his computer and sees the words 'DEBUGGER YOU ARE MISSING A DONGLE', he shouts for Melinda.

There has been a recent survey that says 85% of men no longer consider themselves the most technologically competent member of the household. This has been borne out by our local sample of one – our neighbour's ten-year old son who gravely declared his father not to be 100% when it came to technology. Children are gaining the upper hand. Women, who originally were not at all keen to be sitting in front of a computer all day, are having to step up to the plate vis-à-vis technology so as not to be left behind. In the twenty-first century, it is not virginity you fear losing but your dongle, not your memory but your memory stick. Tweeting, twittering and throbbing are all here to stay so we had better get used to it. The Internet brings with it good and bad and like the axe and the hay-fork, can be used in many ways.

Alan Turing started it all, he who recently received a post-humous apology from Gordon Brown (whose whole life seems to be one great apology). As Gordon said, Alan Turing was quite something – a brilliant mathematician, the founder of computer science, and a strange visionary. Later, in a place called Silicon Valley, inventors, scientists, engineers and entrepreneurs created the high technology revolution and the Internet, amongst a host of other wonders such as mobile radio systems, disk drives, genetic engineering, satellite technology, long distance high voltage trans-mission, integrated circuits, microprocessors, spacecraft health shields, and robotics

Hazel did all the research for this chapter – I am definitely not the most competent member of my family. I daren't ask my son about anything as whenever I pluck up courage to say, 'Can I borrow you for a minute?' he gives me a world-weary look, as only teenagers can, and says, 'You can't want me to show you how to attach something AGAIN.'

However, when we were snowbound and writing this book, Hazel and I were both very grateful to Alan Turing and all at Silicon Valley for creating the super highway that we needed and, like Gordon Brown, we feel very sorry that he was treated so badly after the war. It does seem strange, though, that politicians who were not responsible for the errors of previous governments feel obligated to dish out so many apologies on their behalf. Everything is an epidemic these days and apologies are yet another to add to the burgeoning list.

When they are not busy apologising for themselves or someone in the past, we wonder if MPs are feeling 'at one' with the high tech revolution. During Prime Minister's Questions we noticed someone in the row behind David Cameron passing his Blackberry over so that David could read a blog, e-mail or tweet. Mobiles seem to have replaced cigarettes for those who want something to fiddle with in tricky social situations, Twitter was the chosen medium for Gordon Brown to reveal his biscuit preference: 'absolutely anything with a bit of chocolate on, but trying very hard to cut down.' Is it really in the public interest to know that Gordon feels guilty about nibbling chocolate? With obesity now a bigger threat than smoking I suppose it is.

Rival party leaders have been less reticent about their biscuit predilections: David Cameron likes oatcakes (nice and healthy) while Nick Clegg prefers Rich Tea, if they are dunked, and Hobnobs if not. Is this a case of too much information?

Sarah Brown sent out 1162 messages in 6 months averaging 6 tweets a day. The army of fans listening into Sarah's tweets amounts to almost five times the entire membership of the Labour Party. We know she loves *The X-Factor*, apparently she 'can hardly bear it'. We know so many things that we needn't.

Twitter apparently hasn't made money yet, but it will pretty soon I imagine. (As soon as I write this sentence I read that Dell has made $6.5 million from exploiting Twitter for commercial gain.) My own feeling about Twitter is that it is mercifully brief. What can you say in such a short sound-bite, apart from 'I am on the train'? I must stop being an old fogey, although old fogies are leading the march on Twitter – look at Stephen Fry.

I wonder what Pamela Harriman would have made of it all? She declared 'face to face' was better than 'fax to fax', although she was very canny and if it helped her cause, whatever the medium, I'm pretty sure she would have used it. There is no reason why Twitter can't be mobilised to provide a forum for good causes, as well as the morally dubious. This positive power has already been illustrated abroad, in situations such as the Mumbai bombings and the Iranian Presidential Elections. The day after the Iranian elections, the front pages of Iranian newspapers were covered in blank space where news stories had been censored, but Twitter was still delivering both opinion and key protest information.

In Britain, though, Twitter generally seems to be used by many MPs to bolster their importance, providing us with a running commentary on their lives, almost like a millennium version of the Nixon tapes. And a lot easier . . . what a lot of technology Nixon had in his basement. Not too much to impeach anyone with on Twitter, although only time will tell. Twitter causes no end of scandal for celebrities and footballers, so perhaps it's only time before the Twitter political scandals will multiply. Twitter has already caused trouble for Darren Johnson (London's green chief) when he made the mistake of tweeting from the back of an illegal cab after the City Hall Christmas Party.

I suppose MPs can keep in touch with their subjects (oops . . . electorate), their friends and if they are bored at one of those Home Office working lunches, which cost the taxpayer quite a bit of money but at least keeps the Westminster restaurants open, they can receive tweets from their favourite celebs.

Anyway Hazel tells me the Internet is all abuzz about Twitter. The New York Times calls Twitter 'one of the fastest-growing phenomena on the Internet' . . . it says 'Twitter is a free service which lets you keep in touch with people through the exchange of quick, frequent answers to one question: 'What's happening?'

There is a site called Tweetminster which exists to co-ordinate Internet haikus from our MPs. You don't even have to be there any more, you can just tweet. Tweetminster states proudly that 'it puts the power of Twitter to a noble and valuable use'. It's worrying though – if you actually read the banalities tweeted out by some of these top men it makes you wonder. The dictionary definition of 'to tweet' is 'to utter a succession of chirping sounds'. We are sure MPs could make better use of their time. Do they actually think we are interested in the minutiae of their daily doings? The sad thing is we are. What does that say about us? Unfortunately it says more about us than it says about them.

So is it narcissistic and egotistic or are they, like Trollope's Rattler and Roby, the Liberal and Tory Whips in *The Prime Minister*, just following instructions? We discovered that the Labour Party has issued guidance on how to Twitter. A civil servant has produced a 20-page strategy document on it. Sarah Brown must have been the first recipient. He has advised everyone to spend an hour a day posting between one and ten tweets. So, no more reading *The Times* on the way home or having a nap! Your duty is now to reach out to the electorate in ever new ways. MP's tweets must be 'human' (would that be to include mistakes?) and in tune with the current zeitgeist.

Anyway politicians, or possibly their interns, have gone mad for Twitter – although you can't quite see Anthony Steen and Sir Peter of duck-house fame exactly embracing this technology. Perhaps this is another reason why they are being shunted out. Hazel Blears – yes – it would be a natural extension of her normal conversation. When she and her fellow babes in the Commons were not jumping up and down to catch the Speaker's eye they could be tweeting to Westminster and the world.

For there is no restriction on how or whom you tweet and anyone can choose to become a 'follower'. I wonder how sur-veillance and security deal with this. No tweeting near mosques or churches or synagogues or airports – every tweet must be quality and diversity aware. Don't mention Iraq or Afghanistan or Gaza or anything sensitive. Stick to the obvious: 'made it to baggage claim,' tweeted Craig Fugate, Obama's choice to run the Federal Emergency Management agency, last month. For security reasons I do hope he didn't reveal the actual airport. Who could possibly want to know this information except his wife, although probably not even his wife. Husbands are always too ready to let us know their progress in pursuit of a hot dinner, even before Twitter was thrust upon us.

We received enough of the old-fashioned text messages before Twitter was added. In fact that makes me wonder – do wives become followers or do they prefer to be exempt? Most wives presumably have enough contact with the minutiae of their husband's day-to-day existence, without needing extra updates. Obama himself is said to have 2.6 million fans on Twitter but says he never uses it. How's that for a mixed message?

Still, they are all at it. Boris Johnson and Nick Clegg (remember 'Mr Clegg must be heard') are twitterers. Even John Prescott; 'As Labour's cyber-warrior I am at the cutting edge of modern technology,' quoth he. Jim Knight MP announces to anyone interested that 'he is snowed under with paperwork'; the subtext being 'I am a very busy and important man'. What would it take for him to see that his own situation also applies to others . . .

41

the police for instance (and teachers, his special responsibility). Perhaps he could do something about this, not just complain about his own workload.

MP Tom Harris twitters to say says he 'can't find the TV remote control'. Which, as we know, to most politicians (from the size and style as revealed in the expenses scandal) is like losing their private members and not as in 'bills'. Without TV they are un-manned.

On and on it goes. Surely new media used badly is not the way to re-engage the electorate. John Prescott has said that young people are turning away from politics, but is knowing what JP is watching on TV going to engage young voters? If this is the case, the country is in bad shape.

I wonder how many followers John Prescott actually has. Does he know about SnapTweet? Take note John, and all MPs – Snaptweet sends your latest Flickr photo to your Twitterstream. This is a really speedy method to get your photo out to 'up' your profile. We just hope your profile fits your screen, but if not, using a wide-angle lens would help.

One recent study decided Twitter was pointless babble any-way, 'half-wits and attention-seekers', not our choice of words but you may have heard it here first. However, some serious people like Al Gore send links on Twitter to interesting articles already published. I wonder what proportion of tweets posted during the Copenhagen Climate Summit said 'see you at the Little Mermaid' rather than highlighting interesting articles on Global Warming.

No one wants to be left out of the Twitterati. Christine Hamilton has signed up under the name of Brit Battleaxe – at least, unlike most MPs (she married one), she has self-knowledge. Has she been subject to Twitterectomy? (the removal of someone from the list of people you follow).

I am wondering how dextrous some of these middle-aged MPs might be. If reading glasses can't be found a junior might have to do the tweeting. A disastrous scenario could follow: tweets for constituents might well get mixed up with tweets for the wife or mistress and then who knows what could happen. Facebook is already linked into one in five divorces. I would guess the best advice from either David Cameron or Gordon Brown would be 'take control of your own tweets'. The following list of tweet definitions might prove invaluable too:

Dweet – tweet sent while drunk (after a Home Office lunch say).

Mistweet – a tweet one later regrets (you can't get tweets back remember).

Twadd – to add someone as friend or follower. Best not to do without the glasses.

Twigged out or twired – so hyped on twittering that you can't nod off, even in the Lords.

For those members who still can't fathom it help is at hand. Here is the advice given by Hootsuite, a professional Twitter client: 'Organise your Twitter Stream into friends, news, search terms, keyword tracking [most important in the biscuit arena] . . . whatever you like!' or Track Statistics: 'Impress your friends, your boss or just yourself with our improved visualisation statistics.'

I suppose (reluctantly), that Twitter does give a more personal view of politics, but virtual empires are prone to collapse and I think most people would prefer MPs to focus on serious issues if possible, even if they might be more difficult.

But casting Twitter aside for a moment, let's just go back to blogging or e-mail. The Internet is supposed to be a great tool of communication yet people now e-mail their neighbour at the next desk thus avoiding having to speak to them. As Jane

McLoughlin has said, the new type of friendship function of the Internet 'may lead to a greater level of candour and criticism when comment can be handed out anonymously and without comeback on blogs and chat lines rather than face to face with a real person who might react with anger or distress'. The game 'Football Manager' is to some boys as real as supporting their real life team, only more solitary.

I wouldn't be surprised if Jim Knight found, as well as being drowned in paperwork, his in-box was getting a bit over-full. We all have to deal with our in-boxes as a first priority – if you ignore your e-mail for a few days you are stuffed. Go away for a week and it takes a month to catch-up. In the old days it was the opposite. In Harold Wilson's day, as Bernard Donoughue reports, 'The typing was slow. Nearly every photocopier in transport House not working. Our office out of paper'.

MI5 and 6 glean a huge amount of information from the web. Patrick Mercer MP, chair of the counter-terrorism sub-committee, has warned that insurgents get 80% of their intelligence from Facebook and Twitter. Text messages can be incriminating: the father of the 'syringe bomber' tried to warn the CIA that his son had developed extremist ties in the Yemen – 'Look at the text messages he is sending. He is a security threat.' Officials, presumably overloaded with information and warnings, failed to make the crucial links and Abdul Muttallab slipped through the security net.

After the $40 billion lavished on intelligence reform in the US, eight years after 9/11, how could the same mistakes happen again? As a professor at the University of California said, 'It could only have been more obvious if the guy had worn a T-shirt saying "I'm a terrorist".' Would Jim Knight, for instance, actually know if one of his followers was a member of

Al-Qaeda? Although, presumably the Taliban would not be interested in his latest moves on education for women (if there are any, he's probably struggling to isolate some actual initiatives from all that data).

The thing about technology is that you can literally get tangled up in it. Gordon Brown tried to storm out of a Sky interview but was unable to effect a dramatic exit as he had a microphone fixed to his person.

This is the official advice for politicians worried that their profiles might be messed with: protect your mobile phone with a password (although teenage children, whose own battery has gone flat, and need a phone to send an urgent tweet, will soon get around that). If your phone needs servicing, ensure all photos are deleted (although I thought that phones had in-built obsolescence . . . give an MP the opportunity to get an up-grade and you won't see him for dust, Chris Mullin being the notable exception). Still, it's wise advice if your phone holds photos of your girlfriend and your wife is more technologically competent than you. My ex-husband made this mistake, he changed his password so I couldn't access his computer, not that I wanted to, and then forgot it so he had to get his secretary to retrieve his sensitive messages for him. It's so easily done if you are a man in a hurry, or about to be in big trouble.

Do not become 'friends' with people you do not know or trust. This advice applies outside the world of technology, of course, but in cyberspace it may require a bit of lateral thinking. We all know the Internet can be a dangerous place. Who knows what will jump out to embarrass future Prime Ministers? What would Nick Clegg do if another girlfriend were to suddenly appear on top of the official number of 'no more than thirty' declared women? Check your privacy settings. It's old advice, but politicians have to be tech-savvy to carry it out nowadays.

It's not good though, too much of this sort of thing. Popular culture has laid the foundation for a generation of dysfunctional people to whom the Internet and TV is the most important part of their lives. The poet Louis MacNeice predicted this back in the 1950s. This extract from one of his series of poems called 'Jigsaws':

> Property! Property! Let us extend
> Soul and Body without end:
> A box to live in, with airs and graces,
> A box on wheels that shows its paces,
> A box that talks or that makes faces,
> And curtains and fences as good as the neighbours'
> To keep out the neighbours and keep us immured
> Enjoying the cold canned fruit of our labours
> In a sterilised cell, unshared, insured.

Although these days it seems we are not always supposed to keep out the neighbours: this winter I received advice, along with a thousand others, from my energy provider about how to save on heating. Apparently I should get together with next door one night a week and share a video. So official advice is that we huddle on the same sofa just like the TV Royle family. Brilliant! Be careful if you are invited in to watch anything 3-D though. Those new glasses make a lot of people sick.

We must blame Tony Blair for this enforced togetherness. It all started with Diana. That awful moment in the underpass. I cried. Didn't we all. I was upset for her two sons and the thought that, before the ill-advised Dodie incident, she was just starting to be a respected grown-up person with the work she was doing on landmines, and then all the good stuff was detonated by one drunk driver.

We, women that is, all suddenly became victims and in a way

the martyrhood has never stopped. Diana merged with TV and the media and the media became indistinguishable from government. It WAS government; spin was everywhere. Spin was a more socially acceptable word for propaganda – which sounds too much like Russia and the thought police. Spin is an inoffensive word, perhaps, but not a harmless phenomenon. That ex-rock star of 'Ugly Rumours' fame, Tony Blair, and his chief spin-doctor, Alistair Campbell, used spin to appeal to the public over the heads of Parliament. John Major was horrified: 'Blair's spin is the porn of politics.'

A huge emotional wave spread through the country with Tony Blair its main protagonist. He validated all this gushing and schmoozing. He hobnobbed with celebrity movers, shakers and impresarios and the downward spiral of approval-seeking, reactive government had been set in place – a kind of anti-cerebral, emotional type of government. Image has become all-important. You have to feel sorry for poor Gordon on that front, although thanks to the Biscuit-gate Tweet at least we know he is working on it.

Government ministers now get up early in the morning, not to dash to the House of Commons, but to make their appearances on BBC Breakfast or ITV's GMTV and try to explain government policy. Some important announcements which should really be announced in the Commons are often 'leaked' or trailed on such programmes.

Ever since that moment outside Buckingham Palace when the Mall was filled with flowers in plastic and candles for silent vigil, we've been trying to struggle back to where we were. Once they had their grip on us, the politicians were not at all keen to let go. They had the power and we were on receive. Brainwashing is so much easier if people have less well-developed brains; and since education was on the slide, this was no problem. The important thing was to control the media because that was a good way to stay in power. Indeed some of the images were very powerful; Gordon Brown was Prudence, and by Jove, didn't he look the part – it was all so convincing. How did we go from his prudent way of looking after money to having the biggest budget deficit for over 70 years – £178 billion at the last count.

What had happened to us to create such a fundamental shift? Can we blame Europe? We seem to be getting more and more like the Italians when once we'd been more like the Germans, although of course we never liked the French. What was going on? Or was this sentiment coming from America?

'Loved ones' replaced 'friends and family'; families were suddenly 'hard-working'. An extra adjective here; an epithet there. We were all to wear our hearts on our sleeves to show we were a caring-sharing society in touch with our feminine side. Like the self-help mantra 'because you are WORTH IT', and the great spewing of the life-skill industry encouraging everyone to join 'happiness classes' telling you things you knew already if only you were allowed to trust your own instincts. The obvious was turned into a money-making, money-churning business, preying on the insecurity of the middle classes, offering them something by making them feel doubtful and inadequate. It's all ad-land, if only we could see it.

According to the writers of *The Bumper Book of Government Waste*, the taxpayer foots the bill for a number of 'life courses' intended to help civil servants deal with stress. These included:

Promoting a Participative Team Environment
Self Awareness and Managing Relationships
Develop-Inspire-Achieve

Handling Difficult Situations
Communicating with Confidence
Equality Issues and Responsibility Sessions

One life-skills firm offers piano recitals and cookery courses, which is lovely, but not if it's funded by the taxpayer.

TV programmes, even the BBC, contain subliminal advertising. Subtly in the content where we are supposedly not to notice, or rather not notice, we are noticing. Our short attention spans (which have expedited the success of Twitter) mean that even short programmes recap after the break, or in the case of the BBC, repeat things they have just said. If we can't even absorb half an hour of a Jamie Oliver programme without repetition no wonder teachers have difficulties.

Is TV or Internet life becoming more real than our real lives? It is too easy to retreat into the celluloid Facebook world or the world of 'second lifers' where everything is presented just so. There is an upsurge in Internet porn which is no longer restricted to the top shelf (and the embarrassment that goes with the purchase) or magazines stored beneath the bed. It is now available in staggering quantities at the click of a mouse. Hardly surprising that there is an exponential rise in people addicted to it.

An un-named government official has said that 'Teenagers are risking unemployment because their daily vocabulary consists of just eight hundred words'. They may know a lot more than eight hundred words (well that's a relief) but 'favour teenspeak', which is the abbreviated English they use in text messages.

Strangely, teenagers do not want their parents to see them on Facebook, although the rest of the world is invited in. Compose the line of an e-mail message you really, really don't want to read, asks David Pogue in his book *The World According to Twitter*.

One of the responses consisted of the line, 'Your Dad is now following you on Twitter.' Yes, well. Says it all.

The Internet is seen as safe – there is a distance between people. It is a bit like waving at trains, or hearing about a passenger (now customer) on the line when you are warm and safe inside the carriage. You feel removed, but in this case it is not so. Some of the worst modern atrocities have germinated there and the Internet is now so overloaded with information, it's impossible to filter the rubbish out. It is easy to make catastrophic mistakes at just the click of a mouse.

The *Telegraph* reporters working on the expenses documents had their share of technological mishaps: 'I've just pressed print, and it hasn't sent it to the printer in here. It might have gone bloody anywhere!'

Most MPs do have websites, so you can see what they are up to. Obviously all have a positive spin and there seems to be quite a bit of competition between them, each member vying for bigger and better ones. Journalists, at least those who can actually write, like Michael Gove for instance, tend to have the edge. MPs brief against each other all the time, leaking to the media and using bluff and counter bluff, spin and weave, duck and dive. It's all a game, but hard work trying to gain the upper ground and they daren't miss a trick.

If you actually read all these websites you would never have time to do a proper job. So much of the content is breathtakingly pedestrian – aimed perhaps at those 16–21 olds who aren't in work (nearly a million at the present time). Or perhaps they are designed simply so you can watch TV and tweet simultaneously, facilitating multi-tasking. Anyway there will be less of them soon – the £10,400 budget that MPs were each allowed to spend on websites and self promotion is about to be cut.

The trouble is, what with one thing and another, we do not trust anything we read there, so all the efforts to put out information for our benefit is pointless until some trust can be restored.

Buzz words reign supreme. 'Targets' have been bad news and were found to de-motivate, so are being quietly dropped. 'Managers are one of the biggest threats to workers' mental health', the government advisors (NICE) have said. Bosses are told to 'manage' using praise and reward, not just give criticism. You don't say! Who thought up the idea that good relationships might lead to higher productivity?

Targets also create a groundswell of suspicion – for example, patients wonder if they are being seen because of clinical need or because a box must be ticked. Targets also put A&E Departments under relentless pressure. At the front-line, already they can't cope with any more.

Maybe it would be a good idea to send the people who dreamt up targets on some of that jolly life-skill training? The kind of life-skill training that taps into human nature and the seldom stated but obvious rule that people will only comply with new directives if they are simple, clear and also in their own interest.

Not that businesses took kindly to this advice. They said NICE shouldn't interfere. Strangely NICE, although it is in charge of drugs on the NHS, is also in charge of improving the mental health of the nation. It was the Department of Health that received a Golden Bull Award for saying on a website: 'Primary prevention includes health promotion and requires action on the determinants of health to prevent disease occurring. It has been described as refocusing upstream to stop people falling in the waters of disease.' Hardly surprising that some people prefer the brevity of Twitter.

It is pretty obvious why the advertising industry is burgeoning.

It offers the brightest young people such mega salaries; it is no wonder they don't want to go into teaching or nursing. As Jane McLoughlin says, 'It seems now that everything that happens is a media event, and that's what matters; more than that, if something is not a media event, it doesn't matter whether it happened or not.' It is seen as a profession of people whose job it is simply to work out the angle. And there are jobs a plenty for e-toolers. 'Goggles' is the latest 'facial recognition' tool, although Google seems to have over-reached itself and started it up before it understood the consequences, or in Google speak, 'the implications have been fully explored'.

Google Earth and thousands of cameras on our streets have made surveillance very easy – monitoring our every move. This would have tapped into Harold Wilson's worst fears; he was neurotic about being spied upon and was always summoning people to meetings in remote lavatories so they were in no danger of being overheard.

The government says it will pay for free care for the elderly to stay in their own homes – the £670 million cost being funded by cuts in spending on Whitehall advertising, communications, management consultants and administration. But the government's website is actively recruiting for press officers and administrators. It beggars belief that these costs were allowed to balloon so in the first place. These consultants feed off each other and buoy each other up and they use talented people who could be better employed doing something more useful for society.

How do e-toolers link to the common good? As reported in *The Bumper Book of Government Waste*: 'Curriculum Online' and 'e-Learning' projects have barely dented the public consciousness and certainly not improved education, which presumably was the hope. These projects have cost £430 million since 2002 to set up, including one handout of £350,000 for 'independent product evaluation', meaning a review by a non-departmental public body. *The Bumper Book* authors had a good look at some of these 'evaluations'. Among the failings listed, it identified a low level of awareness of the website, a lack of user friendliness, a bad search engine and problems with using IT hardware. Hardly surprising nobody learnt anything.

This leads to the intractable problem of e-waste such as discarded electronic devices. 'Man held after tonnes of illegal e-waste are exported to Africa,' reads the headline. It's not all hot air – it's indestructible junk silting up our planet, along with so much other stuff.

My feeling is that the government would be better off with a tenth of the present workforce of civil servants, consultants, advisers, e-toolers and general hangers-on. I think it is no more than an expensive kind of social security – it is using taxpayer's money to state the obvious. Whitehall is said to employ 3200 staff in 'information management'; spin-doctors are estimated to cost £300 million a year. That's millions, not thousands, although since the credit crunch we are so blinded by billions and trillions we can no longer visualise quantities.

Mike McCarthy in his book, *Say Goodbye to the Cuckoo*, was fascinated by the language he encountered at Westminster when he was environment correspondent of *The Times* in 1989: 'the idea that you might ring an official directly was greeted with horror, and if you did so you would be referred in short order to the press office'. He was also intrigued by the language of officials: 'It was in effect a private code, which I thought of as "dynamic understatement". A good example would be "unhelpful". This expressed dissatisfaction, irritation, even real anger, in the guise of a sort of rueful acceptance.'

He also observed that the culture of Whitehall was famously secretive and not easy for journalists to penetrate. We certainly found this principle to have remained unchanged when we tried to find a way into the House of Commons ourselves.

It might be 'digital denial' as Arianna Huffington describes it, but I'm not sorry MPs are a bit backward in some ways. Recently Alistair Burt, during a debate, read out a letter from his Blackberry. The Deputy Speaker interrupted him: 'Order. The use of an electronic device for reading from during a speech, I think, I'm not sure that is a good idea.' Bless him!

The Bumper Book of Government Waste also reproduces interesting copy from the Central Office of Information: 'The Central Office of Information (COI) is the government's centre of excellence for marketing and communications. COI works with Whitehall departments and public bodies to produce information campaigns on issues that affect the lives of every citizen – from health and education to benefits, rights and welfare.'

It also conducts research into the sort of people it intends to speak to. Here is an example covering youth culture: 'Common interests for young men include playing and watching sport, going to the gym and cars. They like surfing the Internet, online gaming and Play-station. Increasingly, they 'talked' to their friends in chat rooms, by e-mail, by MSN Messenger or via text messaging. Young women also liked music and were interested in fashion, cosmetics, hairstyles, celebrity gossip and soaps. They talked animatedly about which male stars they "fancied" on TV and in the movies. Young women were also keen on using the Internet for communicating with friends'.

Who can this be for, apart from a load of nincompoops?

Ferdinand Mount is absolutely right that Thatcher's government was 'much less highly propagandist', and the press officers were allowed to simply supply information without spin. Also as Mount recalls, Mrs Thatcher gave far fewer political speeches than Tony Blair and special advisers 'did not bustle about lunching and being lunched, explaining to journalists what brilliant things their ministers were doing'.

Bill Deedes was *in situ* when Alec Douglas Home was made PM and the government came up with a new theme called 'modernisation of Britain': 'It was Deedes' job to come up with a way of projecting this as an exciting new departure for a government that seemed to most observers to be expiring on its feet.' In Bill Deedes' time the government spin operation was pretty compact, consisting of a private secretary and a small staff 'comprising an assistant secretary, an elderly messenger and a driver called Miss Bussey who drove the minister and his red boxes around London and the country'. In fact Deedes found it quite difficult to fill his diary, as in those days 'departments were reluctant to accept well-intentioned advice on presentational matters from the Minister without Portfolio'. Those were the days.

What goes around comes around. While everyone in China wants a car, now we are reinventing the bicycle because of our jam-packed cities. We will wait to see how this parallel virtual universe pans out. Will it be a force for good and raise awareness of important issues or evil, and assist mob rule? It's certainly democratic anyway. Let's hope it doesn't just create a moral vacuum.

3

We Have Ways and Means

Nightmare leaves fatigue: We envy men of action
Who sleep and wake, murder and intrigue
    Without being doubtful, without being haunted.
And I envy the intransigence of my own
    Countrymen who shoot to kill and never
See the victim's face become their own
    Or find his motive sabotage their motives.
                         Louis MacNeice: *Autumn Journal*

It was alleged that when John Major had to make an important decision he took a blank sheet of paper, drew a line down the middle and listed all the pros and cons on either side. Perhaps if Tony Blair had employed this simple methodology he might have realised that war was not such a good idea. For the generation who lived through the two world wars, and indeed most right-minded people since, war is considered to be a very last resort. In the fifties, when the Suez crisis blew up, David Astor, the editor of the *Observer*, wrote in disgust: 'We had not realised that our government was capable of such folly and crookedness. It is no longer possible to bomb countries because you feel your trading interests will be harmed . . . This new feeling for the sanctity of human life is the best element in the modern world.'

One of the reasons that many of us swallowed the apparent

necessity of going to war with Iraq was because Tony Blair was said to have got concessions re 'the road map' towards peace in the Middle East, but this road map, for what is was worth, has languished, forgotten like so many promises. Perhaps it was just a red herring, a distraction. Robin Cook, and in time Clare Short, saw it all for the posturing it was and did the decent thing and resigned. We are no nearer resolving the Israeli/Palestinian conflict, but if the resources had been poured into sorting out this intractable problem, instead of going to war against Iraq, the world might be a safer place.

We would have also been spared three public enquiries and wasted much less public money, and more importantly, lives. Any averagely informed person, that is someone who rarely reads a newspaper and catches TV news by accident, knows that Tony Blair and his intriguers 'sexed up' the dossiers and manipulated facts that were barely open to interpretation, so why more government navel-gazing and hand-wringing? The latest inquiry is like throwing good money after bad. 'Lessons must be learned' my foot!

Why is the government so slow on the up-take? It would be far better to draw a line under the whole terrible shebang. How about, instead of financing the Chilcot Inquiry, we channel the money towards treating children in Iraqi hospitals, or to Headley Court, which is rehabilitating our own soldiers injured in Afghanistan? Afghanistan remains yet another questionable and unresolved conflict. Naturally there is an 'enquiry' (for enquiry read whitewash; after Hutton the words became synonymous). These invariably pointless exercises only serve to undermine public confidence. It's a case of 'don't mention the war', especially not 'regime change'. Except we can't seem to stop mentioning it, like scratching at a wound. 'The bottom line', an expression used frequently by governments, is that nobody thinks any of the wars have made the world safer. We are not safer on our streets because our soldiers are getting killed in Afghanistan, or because we 'won' the Iraq war. Thousands of American forces are still in Iraq, so we haven't really 'won' in any case. And if we want to do any good in Afghanistan we are in for the long haul.

If lawyers must be employed at vast expense it should be to challenge the latest mad governmental sound bite/guarantee/what you will. Ed Balls has promised parents 'a legal right to a good education'. It was part of the Queen's Speech, so pretty important then. But hang on a minute; didn't we all think our children already enjoyed a legal right to education?

We wonder if anyone will contest this. Let's see how it might go? A disaffected parent or group of parents, unhappy with their local school, decide to take the government on. They would go to their local solicitor who shakes his head: it's quite a thing to take on the government. Exactly how can this failure to deliver a good education be proved? To start with you would have to define what exactly a 'good education' is. And nobody knows that, do they? Examination results are forever improving, but nobody believes things are actually getting better. Or at least they can't agree on what exactly counts as 'better'. To challenge the government over this would cost a lot of money and there wouldn't be much chance of returning victorious. The lawyer shakes his head some more, it's all too vague for him, but perhaps he agrees to take on the case. Another day, another dollar.

Most of the parents take fright, but one is more determined. This parent, let's say a single mother on low income, wants to fight on. The lawyer says 'you will need to pay £3000 up front, and there are no guarantees'. There is no legal aid for this kind of thing, since money for legal aid is in short supply. Lawyers were overpaid something to the tune of £25 million in 2008 and although the government is asking for the money back, it is not very likely to get it. So the single parent hesitates.

She manages to borrow the money, but in common with a lot of people employing lawyers, she discovers that her man muddies what she thought were clear waters, and spins things out so her £3000 is spent in two weeks. Her lawyer covers ineptitude with jargon, expects her to do most of the donkey work herself and then sends out a further large bill before she has made any headway. She finds she cannot even have a short conversation with him without being charged hundreds of pounds. And he still shakes his head and blames her when the case founders.

After a while she realises that her lawyer is incompetent. He has taken her for a ride, but she is locked in. She cannot afford to start again. The government knew that if they dragged it out, she would run out of money and steam. The government offer her child a place in another school as a sop. She becomes the subject of a whispering campaign among the other mothers who want their children to go to a better school too. Her child's teacher takes this as a personal attack on her capabilities and freezes the child out. The mother fears her son will now receive an even worse education than before. Her son resents the focus on him and doesn't want to change school, as he will lose his friends. The challenge fails.

Ed Balls is very clever, and was educated among the élite at Oxford and Harvard. It makes you wonder why he spends time writing this stuff. Does he really think anyone will swallow it? Does he even believe it? Perhaps all degrees from whatever the institution are worth exactly the same after all. That *is* something he has made clear.

He knows he is on safe ground though. Resorting to the law for many people can have catastrophic consequences. Legal costs already make lawyers out of reach for the majority of people. The fear of litigation affects every section of society; overzealous health and safety procedures are not usually about risk management but the possibility of bankruptcy. This state of affairs is one of our least attractive American imports and has been discreetly waved in under the radar.

Finally it seems someone is wising up: a headline in the *Independent* on 28 September 2009 read, 'opportunistic city lawyers who overcharge their clients face tough new rules aimed at tackling the excesses and mismanagement of corporate law firms'. We're not going to hold our breath. It didn't take long for the bankers to slip back into their same old ways. Lawyers seem to have been the greatest beneficiaries of the banking crisis. The treasury paid out £107 million of taxpayer cash to city firms to sort out the financial muddle. It has asked for a lot of this back, but so far no dice. Surprise! Surprise!

With bankers in crisis, the city in turmoil, and an election in the offing, now is the time for society to consider just how much it values not just its bankers and lawyers, but all its other professions. Now is the time to review the how and why of pay and remuneration. Much of the expenses scandal was caused by the way MPs expected 'a package' like those taken for granted in the corporate world. The fiddling and ways of fiddling were identical. The suggestion is that unless you work the system for all its worth, you're just a mug. That's what the system's there for, see?

Why for instance should a nurse be paid less than a convey-ancing lawyer? A teacher less than a GP? Why is there such an astonishingly huge discrepancy between what bankers at the top end of the scale are paid and those working in the high street?

Not much 'trickle-down' to be sure. And it always seems to be the teachers and police officers and firemen who suffer most. In 1962 Selwyn Lloyd, then Chancellor, instigated 'the pay pause' and then as now it was the government's own employees who bore the brunt of the financial crisis. Tony Blair once had a strange presentiment; he said: 'If you mess up the finances of the country, it's ordinary people that end up paying.'

Just to remind you how we got into this muddle, and to save the country money on yet another 'inquiry', here is a synopsis: It seems that a lot of risk-taking men took risks that made a lot of easy money and then a lot more sensible men were told by their bosses that they were underperforming if they did not do the same, so they were dragged into it too and they found that despite their reservations they were getting away with it. Although they wondered how long it could go on, they didn't wonder for long enough to stop doing it. And anyway, there seemed no end to it. They were keeping the balls in the air by lending to each other so everything was up, up . . . UP.

Although the men didn't really know who they were lending to, this didn't seem to matter, and in any case it had got a darn sight too complicated to actually fathom. It was obviously working so why worry? Their own contracts were pretty watertight and even if it went a bit wrong, or possibly badly wrong, they knew their personal money was guaranteed and since everyone was doing it, there was safety in numbers and no one person could be blamed.

Even when one or two of these men saw that it was getting a bit hard to actually see how it worked, even for those who were in the thick of it, in fact especially for those (there was a 'wood for the trees' aspect in all this), at least the accountants seemed to know what they were doing. The auditors gave it the nod too because checks and balances put in by governments kept everything above board. If huge companies used a one man bookkeeper from down the street, that was considered prudent good housekeeping (Gordon Brown was once called Prudence remember, and this had always been reassuring), and just a way of keeping overheads down. It was called 'securitisation', which sounds a very safe word. It means bundling up assorted debts, good and bad (apparently you can have good debt), and selling them on to another institution. They in turn sell on until the bank at the end of the chain goes bust. But we didn't know that then. It was quite an eye-opener.

In fact everything was just hunky-dory until some people in America (Harriet Harman says it was men and who are we to dispute this), although it could have been anywhere (but America is the country we went to war with to safeguard our special relationship), started to default on their loans, and men, seeing their debts were being dishonoured by people who had never had any money, or any likelihood of money, and shouldn't have been lent any, let alone what they couldn't afford, started pulling their money out right, left and centre. Without warning.

And because we have gone global and global is good, the disaster began to travel right around the world. It unfolded and unravelled, gaining momentum as it went, like a snowball. Except perhaps snowball is the wrong word, since in business-speak 'The Snowball' refers to Warren Buffett and he was a man who kept things simple, and so kept out of most of the trouble. Warren Buffett is said to be the richest man on earth, and although this may be an itsey-bitsey erroneous since he has also been called an asset-stripper, he does seem to have a small number of staff and be a man who reads thoroughly, trusting his own judgment.

Here in England there was a run on a bank called Northern

Rock which had such a solid-sounding name but turned out to be built on sand, and people got the wind up and were queuing right around the street to get their money out. And this put Gordon Brown into a flat spin. He had to carefully work out his angle and decided to use this disaster to retrench his position and save the world. So he called all the other important leaders, who were also in shtick, and said they should do what he said and more or less they did, for want of any better ideas themselves . . . because this was unprecedented (since the 1930s that is) and they weren't born then and had forgotten their dates as history is taught in a themed way now, and the last great depression hadn't stuck in their memory particularly, even though it wasn't so very long ago.

There was a lot of drama and acting out parts; except that if the men in charge actually went to the theatre, they might know how to look out for these kinds of scams. For example, they might have learnt something from *The Voysey Inheritance*, written by Harley Granville Barker in 1905 and staged by our own National Theatre, a mere 10 minutes from Parliament. The story of Mr Voysey, an investment adviser in Edwardian England who secretly skimmed money from his clients' accounts, could have been an apt warning for all those involved in the Madoff scandal of 2009. Similarly if MPs had read Anthony Trollope's novel *The Way We Live Now*, they might have learnt a thing or two about the nuances of dishonesty and financial scandal. Trollope's book was even dramatised on TV. There's no excuse.

We do know that male MPs, more than they love their wives and constituents, love their TVs, the bigger the better – the bigger the better. Or so they claimed in their expenses.

And here's a sobering thing: it was Linda Davies (a former investment banker turned novelist) who wrote: 'Surely the lawmakers can do something? They have tried but the creativity of the fraudulent and the sheer enormity of their incentives will always be greater than that of the lawmakers.'

Constructing fences is much duller than leaping them.

At the other end of the social scale it is amazing that those who can't seem to hold down a job for whatever reason – inadequacy, depression, simply not being able to manage their lives very well – are inventive in working the system and conning money from the state. They seem to find a way to get every benefit going and find ever more 'creative' (devious and shifty) ways to work the system . . . Remember the case of Shannon Mathews, who had supposedly been abducted? The Mathews family went to extreme lengths to extort money from gullible friends and well-wishers, many of whom were no better off than they were themselves. Karen Mathews was simply trying to cross fences in her own inimitable way. It seems we all love a short cut to riches.

It's a pity they don't all read literature though. It was Scott Fitzgerald who warned: 'at first you go broke slowly and then very fast.'

We need to ask why, apart from nearly making the country bankrupt, do banks also offer such poor service? Has nobody told governments how downright infuriating banks are, as well as flaky? Rather like the credit card statement that warns you 'this page has deliberately been left blank'; in this regard it seems that the government's mind has been left blank.

All the banks in our town are the same. They operate a cartel so the effort in changing your account is not worth the effort. They don't carry foreign currency and are too small to handle coins. They all have do-it-yourself pay in machines so they do not have to do anything for you, really, apart from offering appallingly low interest since the crash. They also have 'new opportunities' on offer. You can have the bother of closing your cheque-free account and opening another with your own cheque book, even though this payment mechanism is supposedly being phased out. This is so you do not waste another customer's time by queuing up to ask the bank to print them for you. They are very responsive to customer feed-back and have found customers have complained about waiting times, so they decided to get rid of the customers. Brilliant! You cannot now draw out a cheque for less than £3,000 or cash for less than £30. That'll show them!

The code of conduct practised at the school for banks (sorry 'University') has also been taught here. It is the art of not catching the customer's eye when having a nice chat and not opening a second window even when a child is screaming and all the old people have collapsed.

Could the government as a prerequisite to propping up the failing and mismanaged banks promise to sort this kind of thing out? Or would this conveniently not be their problem? A local matter we expect. Perhaps due to money-laundering rules and down to Europe? Maybe governments can't interfere in the management of individual companies (this would be heavy handed we suppose and not Free Market), even if the bank is one they own. Or rather we all own.

The best boss we knew was very effective. She worked 8.30 to 4.30 (no unsocial hours), but had an unerring eye for what was important and dispensed with the rest. Her successor worked 12 hours a day, stuffed our pigeon holes with trivia and was far less effective, as well as being considerably more martyred. She would also ring you up at 10.00 p.m. with some minor query and say things like 'I hope I'm not interrupting your favourite television programme', as if this was the only thing she could imagine us doing. We suppose this might well be true of MPs, especially

Gerald Kaufmann whose TV was large and expensive. He says he suffers from an obsessive-compulsive disorder and is a worried kind of chap. Does he know, we wonder, that last year 9,300 people were injured in TV-related accidents? It would be fascinating to find out what proportion of these were MPs.

For success as an MP, as in all important jobs, you need stamina. 90% of success is showing up, but not in the Lords. We don't know if Lord Taylor for instance just clocked on and quickly out again, but his attendance record was just 17.9 %, so not great on this score, in fact not value for money at all. It is known that some members of the House of Lords clocked in just to get their allowances. We know Lord Taylor has a poor memory and is not good at maths. He apparently said he lived with his sick mother in the Midlands till 2007, but the house was sold in 2001 and his mother died that same year, so there was some kind of hanky-panky (or amnesia) going on. The Lords say they don't get paid, yet their allowances are more than many people make in a day, and some people live on this amount of social security for a week. In any case, under new legislation, they are going to be paid £30,000 a year with allowances on top. And it takes brilliance to raise a family on £200 a week, and greater genius still to raise yourself up into daylight and self-sufficiency.

At work a good sense of humour helps, but isn't essential. Mrs Thatcher was known to have no sense of humour. A sense of humour usually involves seeing more than one side of the problem and this kind of vision inhibits action. You can't bang the nail on the head if you are worried about the hammer. Pamela Harriman had no sense of humour either, much as we admire her. More important than a sense of humour is the (rare) ability to sort the wheat from the chaff. More important and rarer still is the ability to think ahead.

Successive governments have failed time after time when it comes to forward thinking. It's partly because they don't have to; they are usually focused on a couple of years until the next election.

Iraq is the most obvious example. Once we were stuck in this war, it might have been a good idea to make provisions for the aftermath; we knew from the Balkans, the Soviet Union and parts of Africa what happens when a dictator is suddenly overthrown. The mafia rules the roost; robber barons with bully boy tactics mysteriously make themselves rich at the expense of everyone else, then abandon their country, change their wives and buy foreign football teams in the spirit of free enterprise.

In addition tribal mayhem, ugly vendettas and civil wars break out to settle old scores and establish the new pecking order. Women, children and old people are caught in the crossfire. More people are sometimes injured in the aftermath of wars than during the war itself. Democracy, which is such an alien concept to many countries, isn't grabbed at like we supposed; there is looting and coercion and corruption. In the urgency to survive and get your bit of the cake, the concept 'hearts and minds' means nothing. In Iraq we doubt there is a Commissioner for Victims and Witnesses paid £100,000 a year.

Another example, this time of a social nature, of governments not thinking ahead and having ideas but no idea about how to implement them, was the year of ROSLA (Raising the School Leaving Age). This was set in motion during the seventies and in 1973 (on Ted Heath's watch) one of us was a new graduate doing a stint of teaching at one of the purpose built, light, airy, open-plan comprehensives. It all seemed very promising but the first thing that went wrong was that we weren't allowed to raise these school children up in any way. We young teachers were taught that on no account were we to impose our own middle-class values on these 'kids' (a word we have always thought patronising).

Unfortunately as we couldn't teach them our values, they ended up with no values at all and precious little education. What we did teach them was themed, and every department had to respond to these 'themes'. If it was 'yellow week' say, Domestic Science (it had moved on slightly from cookery) would introduce custard, scrambled eggs or fairy cakes with lemon icing. English classes would do Wordsworth (daffodils); art classes would paint sunflowers and so on.

The children at this school were nice, kind, not very bright children, but it's doubtful we imparted enough knowledge to last them a lifetime or prepare them for the three-day week or the wave of immigrants which shortly descended on their supposedly bright new patch in the shadow of the old mills and the raincoat factory where their parents worked (and all too soon were to close).

Not that there was much wrong with this teaching method in principle, but team teaching and un-streamed classes need extremely dedicated teachers; it is a first-class system when it operates properly, but this didn't. It wasn't underpinned by enough academic study like spelling, adding up, or fractions, and the open-plan classes encouraged noise and larking about. It was all very friendly, but slack.

The less able boys of fifteen (and for some reason the ROSLA group were all boys although it was a mixed school), instead of going out to work (usually manual of some kind: 'Do you have to be Irish to be a navvy, Miss?') or into apprenticeships or to learn bricklaying at the local tech (now universities), were expected to stay on for more of this (to them pretty pointless) instruction. And they were right; it was pointless. The teacher was supposed to teach them sewing (it was the beginning of equal opportunities whether they liked it or not), so many got round it by teaching them macramé (knots would be at least useful).

These ROSLAs were an encumbrance to the school which, if it had been told how to occupy them, didn't carry out whatever vague instructions it had been given. So they did very little except give most teachers a lot of cheek. 'Hey, Miss, ain't you got big tits, Miss,' or, 'Jack the Plank fancies you, Miss.' Jack the Plank was a small moustached woodwork teacher left over from when the school was a grammar school. He had been sacrificed at the altar of freedom of expression. Boys, instead of sitting firmly behind lathes making stools and pencil cases and being taught to use tools properly, were now running about the open-plan areas with screwdrivers, tripping each other up and waving at the girls making Victoria sponge.

The sad thing was that mixed ability would have worked if we were all brilliant teachers at the top of our game, but we weren't and we failed them. These ROSLA children had an extra year at school but bunked off a lot (who could blame them) and learnt nothing. It has taken nearly forty years for the Tories to have the bright new idea of bringing back Ken Baker to reinstate the technical colleges. Abandon something good and before too long there will be seen a need to reinvent it.

The demise of apprenticeships meant that later there was a huge shortage of skilled labour in most trades. Anyone who can open a paint pot or mend a dripping tap now comes from Poland, which obviously being a less advanced country hadn't benefited from these new educational methods. Now it seems we are being abandoned by the very men who came to help us out. (Note: rather in the way we are training up forces in Afghanistan to run their own army, could these accomplished and hard working Poles pass on their skills, and also their ethos, before they depart?

Before they shut the door could they also explain to the British workman that a dustpan and brush is not just 'for wimmin'?)

Allowing Eastern Europeans in was a godsend to the government when the EU relaxed its borders; so much easier to ship in a trained workforce than battle to motivate our own shiftless youth. Not that these boys we taught weren't willing; they were, but they needed thought and direction put into their lessons which should have made a proper bridge between school and the world of work.

If the government can't think ahead in education, or when it comes to war, what hope is there for global warming? As William Leith has written, 'Societies destroy themselves, but the people in them don't know they're doing it. They just get stuck in a rut, doing the same things they've always done, making them into rituals, religions, and when the religions stop working they carry on with them anyway, thinking something will turn up, because it has always turned up.'

Not that we are disputing that MPs work hard. We asked a young researcher to describe the day of a junior shadow minister. It went from 7.15 a.m.–10.00 p.m., and that was without any kind of late sitting. It was a day lived at breakneck speed; meetings with schools, hospitals, teachers, doctors, dashing to the debating chamber, writing speeches for up-coming debates, dealing with constituency complaints. It seems it is always complaints. You wouldn't contact an MP if you didn't have a problem, unless you want one of them to open a flower show. They certainly belt from pillar to post but how do they decide (are they allowed to decide for themselves, unlike teachers?) which parts of the day are useful to society and are not merely raising their own profile? The trouble is if they are seen to be sitting and thinking they won't be considered men of action. Perhaps that is why Keith Vaz MP is organising a tour of London nightclubs to find out more about class A drugs.

Sometimes the best ideas come from quietness. Take Iain Duncan Smith, although he was ill-suited to be party leader, his social policy report was one of the best things to come out of the Conservative Party for years. He must have pondered for hours on that excellent document. We hope it is still on DC's desk and has not been shredded, or lost, along with our 'Cameron's Cat' film.

When we talked to our own MP, Charles Hendry (a thoroughly good egg), he remarked how many more constituents had contacted him since the advent of e-mail. We asked him about the decrease in hours, actually in the chamber that is, and he said the workload was the same and was simply done differently. He personally regretted the change in hours as there was less opportunity to get to know MPs from different parties (he obviously didn't think that taking all views on board precluded action). He was the only MP we talked to who brought up the question of modernising prisons and doing more in the way of educating prisoners, which might have been surprising in a Tory, but somehow heartening. Maybe the latest new idea 'Red Tory' might have something in it. Jack Straw has recently expressed disquiet about the number of women in prison and it would be good to think there may be useful cross-party dialogue going on. Above all, Charles is certainly the type of MP who gets to the 'essence of the thing'. As Shadow Minister for Energy, he explained that he thought of his job as: 'keeping the lights on'.

It seems to us that everything has got just too complicated; banks, the law, regulation and red-tape of all kinds, and what the next government should be doing is cutting a swathe through everything over which it has jurisdiction.

Flat tax: it may not be completely 'fair' but it has the advantage of being simple to administer and therefore less open to corruption. Think of the hopeless and ineffective chasing up of missing dads by the Child Support Agency. Millions of old people pay too much tax because they simply do not understand the system. And their needs are ignored by banks and building societies that are forever changing their types of accounts and ways of charging. When everybody else has switched to something better (you have to watch banks like hawks), old people are left with neglected and ancient accounts paying low rates of interest. And this was before the credit crunch. Additionally the best deals are on the Internet and this is not easy to access for the elderly.

A flat rate of Parliamentary pay, with just travel expenses added, would also be a good idea. What could be simpler? No need to spend money on think tanks or reviews, or judiciary committees to see if was legal or supportable. A super-saver. You could work it out on a piece of paper just like John Major, and not even have to draw a line.

4

The Brightest and Best

We MPs are in the position of workers at a threatened
factory: if we resist there are thousands of thrusting youths,
clever pillocks and ambitious idiots ready to replace us.

Austin Mitchell

'If you get a seat and were in Westminster during the week, what
would your husband do for sex?'

According to a correspondent in the *Independent* this was a
question asked of a prospective Conservative candidate in 2004.
Now we know the answer . . . rent a porn video and charge it to
the state. In poor Jacqui Smith's case she tried to keep her husband
on stream; she gave him a role (running her constituency office)
and a salary to try to make him feel important, but all to no avail.

She probably knew deep down as every sharp woman knows
that you cannot leave men unattended. You could try to make
them into your wife and do a sort of role reversal, but it wouldn't
really work. They'd always be slipping out to the Post Office (if
there are any left that is), or instructing the blonde researcher.
Hell, what to do?

Husbands take up such a lot of time. You can bet Ann Widdecombe wouldn't have written all those novels if she had a
husband. Tessa Jowell had to give hers up when it was discovered
he was tied in with Berlusconi's dodgy business dealings. He has

gone on record saying that he kept 'Mr Berlusconi out of a great deal of trouble that I would have landed him in had I said all I know.' It is a pity he landed his wife in it instead since her career has never fully recovered.

Mrs Thatcher organised her life pretty efficiently by having twins (no need to do it again), hiring a Norland nanny and making sure that Denis was always on the golf course. You have to admire her. There was no rushing home red in the face because you have two minutes to spare before the nanny goes off-duty, or dashing into Marks & Spencer on the way home and hoping he won't say 'not broccoli again'. Or sellotaping an angel costume at midnight, knowing you have a constituent arriving at 9.30 a.m. and your commute from home is two hours.

Of the female MPs in the Commons (at the 2001 General Election, the number of female Labour MPs dropped to 95), quite a few are single or divorced. You must either have the domestic load taken off your shoulders or not have a load that needs to be lifted. Theresa May is fortunate that her 'best mate in politics' is her husband, who is a 'great supporter' (does he choose her lovely shoes?) but not all female MPs have this great back-up system. In fact many of them seem to have lean, contingent arrangements and struggle to juggle the various parts of their lives.

Ruth Kelly bucked the trend by being married and having four children while she was an MP but she is on her way out now, not just out of government; she has resigned from Parliament full stop. We hoped she could hold her own. We women watched with baited breath, but somehow we knew it couldn't be done, and actually we feel relieved, even unburdened.

Still, back in the kitchen with four children, she may occasionally look back with nostalgia to those quiet cabinet meetings when helpers would bring her coffee in a special mug. And we don't think she will find she is a 'non-working' mother either. Despite government's efforts to help her back into the workplace, she might find with all those children she is 'working' quite hard where she is.

There were no two ways about it, Ruth Kelly, in particular, got a very raw deal as a minister. She was taunted and bullied by other MPs and persecuted by the press. They picked at her religion, her children's education, her house-husband that wasn't. Whatever she turned her hand to, it seemed she failed in some way or other. She was also constantly being reshuffled and before she could get a grip of her brief, a crisis would brew, and there she was back in the limelight.

If we were Ruth Kelly we'd have given up long ago. One of us knows exactly what we'd do; we'd move to a sparsely populated county like Herefordshire where there were still some good local schools and offer to curate something wonderfully esoteric like the National Snowdrop Collection. It might be difficult with small children (we used to pay ours not to help in the garden), but at least we could make as many mistakes as we liked without them being beamed back to the *Daily Mail.*

As Harold Macmillan knew only too well, 'politics is not just a difficult trade but above all not for the faint-hearted. In fact, it is only for those who have the will and who are, at the same time, able – by being, in truth, self-centred – to surf the waves of hostility which they will encounter.'

Dr Thomas Stuttaford, writing in *The Times*, took it one further. He wrote about the type of personality that has always been associated with power and climbing the greasy pole. He described it as 'those who have an underlying sociopathic personality, a phrase that is no longer medically acceptable. These are people who live just, but only just, within the rules laid down by society in which they exist. They have a love of excitement and of a colourful, if superficial life. They are manipulative but also impulsive, can be reckless with their own safety and that of others, and are frequently irritable and aggressive if frustrated. Their regard for truth is variable; unfortunately they tend to include politics with love and war as areas in which a lack of honesty is acceptable.' Well that explains the expenses scandal then. And a lot of other stuff.

There has been a recent survey that points out that 'bad doctors are overwhelmingly men'. In fact, as Jeremy Laurence writes in the *Independent* (and I imagine Harriet Harman would agree), women are far safer: 'They are less likely to be investigated by concerns over their behaviour, clinical skills or conduct and are significantly less likely to be suspended or excluded from work than their male colleagues.' We wonder if this would also apply to male MPs . . . no actual scientific evidence of course, but it's tempting to wonder.

Obviously you need a lot of different qualities to become an MP and of course it helps to have a bit of derring-do, but not too much if Dr Stuttaford is right. It would also help if they had some history and English at their fingertips, Shakespeare would be especially useful: '*all the men and women merely players: / They*

*have their exits and their entrances; | And one man in his time plays
many parts.'*

From what we could see from our official tour of the House of
Commons, middle-aged male MPs seemed to be teamed up with
younger women. No mathematical evidence of course (although
we would never let the lack of a spread sheet get in the way of
making a hypothesis), and it could have been a statistical anomaly,
or perhaps all the young men were simply on holiday in August.
There seemed to be a certain amount of cloning of those that
were scattered about. What could these metro-sexuals know of
life beyond Westminster?

There have always been a scattering of female MPs like Barbara
Castle, but the sea-change occurred in the Blair landslide of
1997 when Labour ushered in 101 female candidates for the
first time. Some of these women have fallen by the wayside in
one way or another, but many have hung on. The disappointing,
and also perplexing, thing is they don't seem to have changed
things as we expected and also they allowed us to go to war
on very flimsy evidence. Blair seduced them and us with his
'Education, Education, Education' promise yet failed to deliver,
as in so much else.

It was a surprise that Blair's Babes made so little impact. If you
look at the Commons from above it still appears predominately
male. Women managed to change the hours to be more supposedly female friendly, but it was just a bit of tinkering. Besides,
there are plenty of jobs and professions in which your work goes
on into the evening: teachers, doctors, cleaners; or if you are
running your own business or doing deals with foreign countries
in a different time zone. It wasn't so revolutionary. As Charles
Hendry pointed out the workload is no different, whatever the
hours.

Sometimes in politics, as in war, the advance guard doesn't make the most impact; perhaps we will have to wait for a second surge of Conservative ladies to make a difference. As Avril Gillies, a Tory activist from Scarborough said: 'We hope the men can be dragged kicking and screaming into the twenty-first century.' Tory ladies, who in the 1980s still wore hats to conference, have always been a force to be reckoned with.

David Cameron has only nineteen women MPs at the last count so he has to be inventive and try out different techniques of putting women in place. It is a fact that if you don't have all-women shortlists there will be fewer women MPs and fewer female concerns will be debated

An opportunity to experiment came sooner than expected. Somebody at Tory Party HQ had the idea of holding an open primary at Totnes. David Miliband has now said that Labour might do something similar – such a copycat. Anthony Steen, a disgraced Tory MP (expenses), had a hissy fit and stood down (he was over seventy and had had a good run) and David Cameron saw a chance to strike while the iron was hot.

He put in place Sarah Wollaston, an attractive female candidate, a political ingénue but a highly thought-of local doctor and, lo and hey presto, she was elected to be the prospective parliamentary candidate in this very safe Devon seat. It is a kind of progress as until now the electorate has always had candidates chosen for them by a small group of party workers.

But it is still an uphill struggle; not everyone is pleased with Cameron's great new ideas. Local activists in Beckenham are fed up that they are expected to have three women candidates out of a shortlist of six. They've considered it their right to fix local contests up till now. Although these women include a scientist (and that is a type of candidate that we need more of, particularly those who are able to interpret statistics and not take them just at face value) and a writer . . . (a writer, no wonder they are sniffy!).

Peter Dean, a local Beckenham councillor who knows his mind, said, according to the *Telegraph*: 'Frankly the calibre of women was very poor.' Rather at odds with Harriet Harman's declaration that 'men cannot be trusted to run things on their own'. Activists are apparently campaigning energetically for an ex-Bosnia commander, presumably because he sounds as if he would have more authority. At local level there is often distrust of intellectuals, they prefer people who look like 'doers'.

Still you do have to feel a bit sorry for these local party members; the carpet has been wrenched from under them and it is no fun delivering leaflets in the rain and getting people to hang signs in their apple trees. They used to pride themselves on being free from meddling from above. And now they've been told they're not to mind about extramarital affairs! 'Having an extramarital affair should not stand in the way of someone becoming an MP,' declaimed Baroness Morris of Bolton. It must be a bit hard to swallow.

Ann Widdecombe has always taken it for granted that she was equal to the male MPs because 'we all got there on the same basis', but Theresa May has pointed out, as only she can, that 'we've had all-male shortlists in the past. Nobody said they were "discriminatory, patronising or ineffective".' Something of a U-turn here: back in 1997 Theresa May firmly stated that she had become a candidate on her own merits and had no burning ambition to promote women's parliamentary rights.

We happen to know that Theresa was dressed in matching blue jacket and skirt when she uttered these last words. Reporters just love to tell us how women look . . . they simply can't stop themselves. Can you imagine a description of Eric Pickles canvassing in

Theresa's shoes

a charcoal suit with a subtle pin stripe, possibly from Marks & Spencer, or attending London Fashion Week? Katy Bourne, a would-be Conservative aged forty-five, was called a 'cutie'. In fact all new Conservative candidates have been labelled 'Cameron's cuties'. Do we see Michael Gove as a cutie? Charles Clarke? The possibilities are endless.

The latest kerfuffle (although by the time this book is out there will be plenty more) is happening in North West Norfolk. It is the Conservative Party versus Sir Jeremy Bagge and caught in the crossfire is the hapless candidate, Elizabeth Tremlett. Sir Jeremy has got in a froth because he doesn't want a candidate foisted upon him. It has nothing whatsoever to do with her being a woman, of course. Sir Jeremy has made it quite clear he has nothing against women: 'Who cooks my lunch? Who cooks my dinner? How did my wonderful three children appear?' he said in a *Sunday Telegraph* interview. Sir Jeremy wasn't the same man who thought up: 'Make her feel special with a clothes line', was he?

When all this came up we were reminded of a passage in John Rae's book *The Old Boys' Network*. Rae was trying to get to the bottom of a plot in which a girl new to the sixth form (in an otherwise all-male Westminster School) was being bullied and humiliated. He deduced what was behind the incident: 'Resentment on the part of these boys at the ease with which the clever girls in general and this clever girl in particular, sail to the top of the class.'

As one Sussex headmaster, whose school was about to go co-ed, said to us not so long ago: 'We can't have 50/50 . . . too many girls and they would simply *takeover*.'

It is said that there are worries that clever twenty-seven-year-old Chloe Smith who won the Norwich North by-election . . . may be 'promoted too fast'. Remember the furore when Lady Aston got the highly prized European job. 'Who was she?' they all spluttered. 'She must be useless if nobody's ever heard of her.'

Iain Hollingshead's book *Am I Alone in Thinking* . . . is an anthology of letters that didn't quite make it on to the *Telegraph*'s Letters Page. Here is Gloucestershire's version of Sir Jeremy Bagge:

Sir – I am not sure where it all started, but can we please rid the BBC's rugby coverage of female commentators. They have not the slightest idea about what it is like to play the game, and so their comments are worth nothing. Listening to ignorant money-earners is no replacement for listening to chaps who know what they are talking about.

Lt Col Dale Hemming-Taylor (retd)

We do have a soft spot for these men. Their world has been upturned and it's just not cricket. You can see why so many of the old Tory Guard who are being swept out by David Cameron feel aggrieved. Luckily, harrumphy old buffers are popular on TV at

Charles Clarke

least; you only have to look at John Sergeant of *Strictly Come Dancing* fame. It is not commonly known that Tim Loughton and Peter Bottomly, Sussex MPs, tabled an early day motion which said: 'This House is devastated by the circumstances surrounding John Sergeant's departure.' It is good that this section of society is being preserved in aspic (or celluloid). Could part of it be that these MPs know that one day they will be harrumphy old buffers themselves?

Still, you need all types in Parliament; moral philosophers as well as mavericks there to get things done. However carefully you assess candidates, male or female, there are bound to be some surprises. All organisations have their members who look good on paper but don't come up to scratch. It would be surprising if Parliament was any different. As usual Trollope has them off to a T. The foreword to the Oxford University Press edition of *The Prime Minister* explains: 'Rattler and Roby are the Liberal and Tory Whips and embody the principles of blind party loyalty and cynical expediency, Fitzgibbon is notoriously lazy, and Macpherson illustrates the rewards earned by loyal voting rather than hard work.'

We know who *you* are, thanks to the *Daily Telegraph*!

Not all MPs are any more pleased with their constituencies than their constituencies are pleased with them. Harold Macmillan thought his ' . . . a truly dreadful prospect. I have scarcely been near Stockton for five years. I have no agent, no association and no funds! It seems my fate to try to get away from Stockton, but never achieve it.'

Roger Scruton believes, in common with many others, that MPs should not begin their careers in politics, but should come to politics from some other walk of life. He saw politicians' greatest defects were those that arose from professional politics itself: meddlesomeness and half-education. Rather like Anthony Trollope he believed 'they should regard legislation as a painstaking procedure, and a solution of last resort to conflicts that ought if possible to be settled by other means'.

It seems, from a cursory glance at the list of female candidates lined up by David Cameron, quite a few are emerging from the world of PR. It is hardly surprising. These women will have the skills of presentation and image at their fingertips, although they all look very coy and girl next door-ish in their publicity photographs. Elizabeth Truss looks particularly winsome in gold; it's easy to see why MP Mark Field fell for her.

Do these women dressed in peach and apricot have what men would call 'the equipment' to hold their own in the Commons? Not that the Tories were not entranced by Mrs Thatcher. As well as seeing her as a defender of private enterprise and the free market economy, they also saw 'a queen-like figure in black taffeta'.

It is important that older women should not be overlooked as possible candidates. In our local Waitrose it is the sixty-something women who are giving the clear directions; the men of the same age are often lurching about, not quite in control of their trolleys. In the 1980s, Teresa Gorman (what a lot of Teresas there are in Parliament) had to lie about her age to be accepted as a candidate, and later was vociferous in promoting Hormone Replacement Therapy as a way in which women could keep up their energy levels. Older women may not be chatted up, but they have a right to be heard. And they are less likely to have affairs or roar off on motorbikes. (Warning! The young and pretty turn into battleaxes in the end.)

A funny leaflet (as in funny-peculiar) arrived not so long ago. It seemed to have been typed on an old Remington and possibly even Roneo'd, as it had missing letters and ink-splats and rambled on in the usual English-nutter kind of way. (In the olden days these pamphlets would have been distributed outside Woolworths on a Saturday morning.) It warned of a feminist plot to create a new form of political society where 'wOMEN DOMINATE' (*sic*) rather than where harmony exists between the sexes. Apparently 'girl-power' was coming in through the back door of the EU (squeezing in next to farming subsidies and more health and safety legislation perhaps?) We still seem far off from this future horror, but it does give some indication how women are still, in some quarters, very much feared.

Although we're in favour of promoting women and their rights we don't think toddlers belong in Parliament. All those sticky fingers on the lovely gold statues. So many hazards and no-go areas and alarms that could go off. Babies may occasionally be useful for canvassing, but they are a distraction in the workplace. Of course it's nice to take them in once and show them off, but that should be it. We may be wrong but we don't remember seeing any baby-changing facilities on the grand tour.

We don't think it is at all easy to be a good MP. If you have very young children and you value your health and sanity, then it shouldn't even be attempted. There are so many potential complications: if you leave the nanny in charge, she may run off with your husband; if you leave your husband in charge, he may fall asleep; and good-will from your elderly parents can turn to ill-will if they are called upon too often.

We are all going to live so long now that it would make much more sense to offer your services to the country before and after you have children. Great insight and wisdom is gained while raising a family. It is not a fallow time and you have much to offer when this is done. If we are all to live to be ninety, taking ten or even twenty years out for child-rearing does not seem long.

Women are adept at reinventing themselves and adjusting to circumstance. Versatility is in our DNA.

Every time there is a scandal there is a resurgence of the celebrity MP. Esther Rantzen is the latest television chat show personality to charge to the rescue, in this case of Luton South, whose own MP (a one time Blair babe) has gone off sick with expenses problems. Esther will add a bit of razzmatazz on election night I suppose.

Trollope (yup, him again, our guru) thought politicians were there to entertain, and they don't disappoint. Some of the best cinema (*In the Loop*) and TV dramas have been inspired by or have actually recreated the adventures of our MPs. There was *The Long Road to Finchley*, dramatising Maggie Thatcher's rise to fame, and a very funny sitcom about John Prescott's high jinks at Chequers. Later it was followed by a no less funny documentary of Prezza and Pauleen touring the British Isles intent on proving our divisive class system is in fine shape even after years of affirmative action (equality and diversity) by Prescott's own government. He even has a new green agenda. Is this some kind of redemptive act to carbon off-set his two Jags? And 'coming out' as a bulimic? Was this late onset empathy with Diana, or advertising for his latest book?

MPs have much in common whatever their political persuasion – huge egos, worries about position in the tribe, whether they still have time to make a mark, anxieties about being overlooked by superiors and so on. Our outreach worker at the Conservative Party Conference said that the whole place was surging with testosterone. Could this be the threat of all those 'thrusting', 'clever pillock', and 'ambitious' *female* candidates ready to step up to the plate?

5

Wives and Mistresses

'Power is the great aphrodisiac.' So said Henry Kissinger. Well it can't really be looks can it? Not if the public gallery is anything to go by.

When we heard about John Prescott's Tracey on the radio there was a rush for the *Daily Mail*. 'What did she look like? What made her do it? What can she have been thinking of?' On the back benches beauty is obviously in the eye of the beholder and at least their mothers love them, but (and there is much supporting evidence in a recent scientific study) it seems that men are not getting any more attractive. They are also still fallible human beings that cheat and cover up, although this aspect didn't need to be surveyed.

Paul Marsden MP, a floor-crossing Lib Dem and one his party seems to have dispensed with unless he has gone to ground, has

gone on record as saying 'the house is full of coke-snorting, alcohol-soaked, totty-chasing MPs'. He said, 'Westminster is fabulous if you want to wine and dine someone. It's easy to sweep someone off their feet. You can show them where Charles I was sentenced to death.' He also said MPs 'stalk the corridors of power late into the night seeking sexual encounters with an ever-willing army of nubile young researchers'. As Anthony Trollope once said, 'Where there is a woman in the case a man cannot be expected to tell the truth.' Well, not the whole truth that is.

According to a recent Grant Thornton poll, 24% of married men would cheat on their spouse if there were no chance of being rumbled.

It's not the cheating that is most disliked as far as MPs are concerned though – it's the hypocrisy.

David Curry MP, chair of Parliamentary Standards and Privileges, was quite circumspect about his particular love triangle (wife and local headmistress), which probably wouldn't have come to light if his wife hadn't forbidden him from staying at the cottage where he'd once stayed with the headmistress (funded by the taxpayer).

The incumbent MP in Ashford, before Bill Deedes, was one E. P. Smith who only stayed three years. The reason (or one of them) for his standing down was that he had a mistress in London for whom he planned to leave his wife, which in those days wouldn't have gone down well in rural Kent. As Stephen Robinson relates in his biography of Deedes, 'Smith glossed over his infidelity in his letter of resignation, pompously noting, "There is something to be said for a man devoting his last act to his home, his family and his more personal and intimate interests." '

Taking pride of place on the scandal sheet is John Profumo. We all remember Profumo. He had a short affair with Christine Keeler, which had long ramifications. According to Philip Larkin, this orgiastic summer of 1963 was the year sexual intercourse began.

The Keeler story was very complicated, and although it was all over the press, it was hard to find out who had slept with whom, let alone the when and the why. Both teenagers at the time, we still remember adults talking about it in hushed, shocked tones. The tale had terrific ingredients – not just sex, but espionage as well: Keeler was supposedly having pillow talk with a Soviet naval attaché. And then the fixer, Stephen Ward (a strange combination of painter and osteopath), committed suicide. There was an official inquiry that concluded no secrets had been leaked (although we now know that is what government inquiries usually say). Keeler was not sleeping with Ivanov and Profumo simultaneously (boring) and, in any case, being a bit dim and dizzy she was unlikely to remember details of nuclear technology.

Valerie Profumo was said to have behaved like a brick and as soon as she heard what her husband had been up to said, 'Oh darling, we must go home just as soon as we can and face up to it.'

Lord Hailsham, formerly MP Quentin Hogg, spoke of 'a squalid affair between a woman of easy virtue and a proven liar'. You have to hand it to Profumo, though, he spent the rest of his life making up for his big mistake and redeemed himself by genuinely useful charitable works. This is a far cry from today, when there would be a quick apology, a few weeks rustication and then an immediate return to the ranks.

Still, the political damage had been done. Harold Macmillan found the whole business distasteful (two of his other ministers, Ernest Marples and Duncan Sandys, were implicated in other minor sex scandals during his premiership) and his own wife had been having a long-running affair with another MP, Bob Boothby, so it was hardly surprising he was jolly fed up.

Dorothy Macmillan, whom Harold loved, is very like Lady Glencora Palliser in Trollope's *The Prime Minister*, a free spirit who subjected her husband to many trials and tribulations: 'You are what you have made yourself, and I have always rejoiced that you are as you are, fresh, untrammelled, without many prejudices which afflict other ladies, and free from bonds by which they are cramped and confined. Of course such a turn of character is subject to certain dangers of its own . . . ' shades of our own Pamela Harriman.

It seems that MPs are always in trouble with women. Anthony Lambton was Parliamentary Under-Secretary for Defence under Edward Heath. In an interview with Robin Day he said, 'Does it matter if politicians visit prostitutes? Surely all men visit whores.' Well, obviously not if their wives or mistresses have anything to do with it, but Parliament is set up for the perfect weekday alibi, although this may be slightly scuppered now that all-night sittings have been abandoned. Although Chris Mullin (there is no suggestion that he ever visited a prostitute) wondered what to do with himself when everyone pushed off early. Lord Lambton told an MI5 official that the sheer futility of his government office had driven him to frenzied bouts of 'gardening and debauchery'. Anyway Lord Lambton resigned, along with Lord Jellicoe who was involved in something similar.

The answer to Lord Lambton's question should be, yes it does matter, as 'sex-working' is degrading for women, and prostitution is linked with people-trafficking, drug addiction and enslavement. In today's world, when taboos seem wholly abandoned, anyone saying 'yes' has come to be considered prudish. Especially as prostitutes have been re-branded as sex-workers, as if that makes them more matter of fact and somehow less sleazy.

MPs are in an extremely tricky predicament. Each and every party bangs on about 'back to basics', family values and so on, so we all think it a bit rich that the rule for ordinary mortals doesn't seem to apply to them. The trouble with the high ground is you can be shot at from above and below, and as men know, being grabbed from below can be very uncomfortable. In general they fall short, very short, of their own high standards when it comes to sex and money.

John Cordle MP blamed money for the sexual profligacy, although he was a Poulson associate and later forced to resign in dodgy circumstances, hoisted by his own petard you might say (before petards were subject to Health and Safety regulations – it could never happen now). 'The wind of change in our affluent society has brought in its wake a gust of lust,' he opined. There was still a lot of pomposity about in the 1960s.

In any case all was not quite as hunky-dory in the Cordle household. His first wife Grace sought to have him jailed for breaching a custody order that he wriggled out of by pleading parliamentary privilege. At the terminal stage of his second marriage to Venetia he imposed a seven o'clock curfew on those visiting his wife and posted security guards to prevent his mother-in-law from coming to stay.

It is virtually unknown for a man to say, 'I think we should separate,' or, 'I wish to live alone for a while to work out where things went wrong.' Well, perhaps not unknown for him to say it, but completely unknown for it to be the truth. A man always has something up his sleeve, some kind of back-up plan, rather like MPs with small majorities. The occasional exception to this rule is when his wife bolts unexpectedly. He then taps into pornography and Internet dating, where he can spell out his needs and wants without any inhibition. With 'equal opportunities' some women have started to behave in the same way.

Women who target younger men even have the name 'cougars' and perhaps this is why Iris Robinson (with a name like Mrs Robinson, it was an accident waiting to happen) had the idea for her affair; she was MP for Strangford in Northern Ireland and had a fling with an apparently willing nineteen-year-old boy. Unfortunately she secured him a loan and her husband found out and the shit hit the fan.

Husband Peter, Northern Ireland's First Minister, appeared on TV forgiving her sexual trespasses and let it be known that God had forgiven her too and that he (not God) needed six weeks off work to deal with things. One observer said she was 'a wee bit flaky' but that he exercised 'absolute control'. Anyway, he occupied hours of prime-time TV sanctimoniously forgiving her and summoning God and looking very grave, making it abundantly clear to anyone who was interested that his wife had been a very bad girl.

Morality is a complicated business: Tony Blair was the soul of probity in his private life, but started a war and sent thousands to their deaths. Just because you restrict yourself to your wife (five times a night according to Cherie) doesn't mean you are a better person exactly, or have better judgement.

And the converse can be true. Robin Cook, a well known 'love-rat', admitted to his latest affair at Heathrow when he was about to set off on holiday with his wife. Someone from Labour head office told him to make up his mind between wife and mistress pronto as it would soon be all over the tabloids, but he was the only MP sufficiently honourable to resign from the government at the outbreak of the Iraq war. And he was one of the first MPs 'to worry about his carbon imprint'. It was rumoured that Gaynor (mistress, second wife) was not allowed to turn any lights on in his flat until he arrived.

Even though MPs do not live up to their trumpeted-about image, there is much we can learn from them, and not just how to keep your mother-in-law at bay. David Mellor proved that you no longer needed good looks to acquire a mistress and Cecil Parkinson demonstrated that looks do not guarantee reliability, as Sarah Keays and her badly-treated daughter were soon to find out. His wife Ann turned into a kind of gatekeeper wife after this, the kind enjoyed by many MPs (wife-secretaries usually assume this particular default position). Apparently Parkinson dithered for ages between his wife and his mistress, which is not the kind of clear and decisive action you might expect from your MP.

Although of course we expect too much. They are really just like us. Consult *Who's Who* and you will see how they try to identify with us, even though they probably think of themselves as rather better. Ed Balls' entry lists playing football and the violin to get the balance right between intellectual and man of the people. His wife, MP Yvette Cooper, says she likes watching TV soaps.

Boris Johnson's wife has sensibly kept her own counsel regarding Boris's many misdemeanours, although she did lock him out in full view of the waiting press while he was wearing a pirate headscarf – surely the best way to react to infidelity. Better than shouldering the blame, rushing to the gym or posing for a family photograph at the gate of the modest constituency home – or more likely very large country house (much more was revealed during the expenses scandal other than mere expenses).

Unfortunately if you are a wife, you can't do right for doing wrong. There is nothing guaranteed to make your husband dislike you more than behaving well when they have behaved badly. Men hate being felt sorry for, or being made to hide. It is a well-known fact that secretaries commonly double as mistresses. However daring and dashing politicians think themselves to be, when it comes to women they tend not to look very far, especially as the new woman will start in a nicely subordinate role. And when it comes down to it, it's only what we know already: doctors sleep with nurses, photographers with models and MPs with their secretaries.

In any case, it isn't always plain sailing. Some of the secretaries are quite a handful. Marcia Falkender, Harold Wilson's secretary and fixer was a terrible dominatrix. As Bernard Donoughue writes in his diary: 'The basis of her aggressive power lay in the realisation by her victims that she could normally mobilise the support of the Prime Minister for whatever she accused or demanded. Without that backing her style would have been less effective, indeed counterproductive and unacceptable in any normal working or social context'. 'He [Wilson] loves it when she shouts at him, corrects him, opposes him'.

His wife was still waiting in the wings though. As Bernard Donoughue also says, 'He will need Mary. She has the kind of solid north-country virtues which can be relied on to be there and support him when the hangers-on have deserted the ship'.

Lord Tebbit's wife, Margaret, was nearly killed for being an MP's wife in the wrong place at the wrong time. She was very, very unfortunate to be caught up in the IRA Brighton bomb plot of 1984 and spent her life in a wheelchair. It was the most terrible bad luck.

It is particularly hard to be the wife of the leader of the opposition. Who could blame Betsey Duncan Smith for admitting that she couldn't wait to get back to ironing shirts, given the flack dished out to her when her husband was leader. We were completely on Betsey's side, and sure she deserved her stipend as his secretary, even if she did answer the phone from her kitchen while she was draining the pasta.

As any wife of an 'important man' will tell you, multi-tasking means ensuring that the Bolognese sauce doesn't stick to the bottom of the pan whilst answering your husband's vital phone-calls. And in the case of MPs' wives you have to factor in all that to-ing and fro-ing from the constituency, finding lost things, telling white lies, passing on vital messages, collecting dry-cleaning and easing the general path of important business. Of course wives should be paid.

There are other interesting facts thrown up by MPs: who would have thought you could conduct a secret affair within weeks of a new marriage and that it would be possible to organise romantic weekends including a child, a special constable and a dog. Kimberly Quinn, what a strategist. Did she go to Harvard with Ed Balls? She was focused, paid great attention to detail, knew how to play the field, and didn't lose sight of her objective. She'd be useful to turn around a failing system or two. She even knew how to maximise her fertility chance – sleep with as many men as possible.

Also, when she achieved her objective, how did David Blunkett MP visit her and his 'little lad' in hospital without bumping into her husband, Stephen Quinn, who thought the child was his? Such a juggling act. We suppose it all seemed so far-fetched and improbable, a bit like a government white paper – at first nobody believed it.

Nobody believed Blunkett either, when, as Home Secretary, he denied that he had fast-tracked the visa for Kimberley's nanny, although Sir Alan Budd's enquiry into the matter (how much did this cost the public purse?) concluded that no one could determine whether Blunkett had given any instructions in relation to the case and if so what they were.

Kimberley bore an uncanny resemblance to Monica Lewinsky, who Clinton was nearly impeached for his involvement with. It can hardly be argued that Clinton abused his power, as Monica was obviously complicit, although unsurprisingly it angered Hillary. Anyway the point was, after Jennifer Flowers and so on, it can hardly have been a shock to the American nation, so why the ridiculous attempt to bring him to trial?

However, one sexual encounter can have major political ramifications. As Yasmin Alibhai-Brown has hypothesised: 'One could argue that if Bill Clinton had not been exposed as a serial philanderer, if he had not desecrated the hallowed White House with his indiscretions, the Democrats might have had a more overwhelming victory with Gore. George Bush junior would then not have claimed the crown. We would not have had the neo-conservatives in power and we would not have had the illegal war in Iraq, and the bedlam which is now set inexorably to follow.'

It is also arguable that if Ted Kennedy (sins of omission, married at the time) had saved Mary Jo Kopechne from drowning, and not kept quiet till the next day about the car being in the river, he might have become President.

Before the war, mistresses were very much looked after and considered part of the holding of power. David Margesson, who was chief whip in the House of Commons when Pamela Harriman was a young woman, knew how important this was. As her biographer Christopher Ogden noted, 'Margesson knew everything that was going on. He knew the details of every political initiative and the strengths and foibles of every politician in every party. He knew who was loyal, who was smart, who had a drinking problem, and the telephone number of mistresses in the event an errant MP had to be summoned for a vote.'

Bill Deedes proved you can still have a romantic friendship in your nineties, even when cathetered up, and also that you can have an affair of a kind without actual sexual congress. He wisely kept this kind of thing quiet until he was out of office and much of it didn't really emerge until his biography was written.

That's the other thing to bear in mind – the truth will out. Love children will eventually appear. Tim Yeo, Clare Short (thankfully Clare would not now be obliged to give up her child – bastards being the norm today, rather than a secret shame) and Stephen Pound have all discovered theirs. We must be thankful that we now have a society in which babies do not have to be hushed up. It has been alleged that even in the twenty-first century Senator John Edwards, a one-time would-be President, asked a friend to pretend paternity of a love child.

We have come a long way since the seventies when Marcia Falkender had two children by a married man. The married man, Walter Terry, was supposed to divorce his wife, marry Marcia for two years, then divorce her and go back to his wife – all in the name of respectability.

We'd all like to be happily married, but probably the best we can hope for is serial monogamy and marriage is often with the compromise candidate. Like so many a white paper there is such a difference between aspiration and reality. 'Pamela Harriman was a pragmatist,' said her biographer. 'If she had married Nelson Rockefeller she would have been a Republican; if she had married Frank Sinatra, she'd have been running the gambling lobby.'

Politicians in particular should remember there is nothing private about e-mail; remember the secretary and the boss ketchup incident? Press the wrong button and e-mail can be sent accidentally or accidentally-on-purpose to the wife, the boss or the whole world. With the Internet, there is still a paper trail – follow the money to find the sex, or vice versa.

One sure way to keep out of trouble would be to steer clear of Annabel's – the nightclub responsible for Blunkett's downfall. David Davis was caught here with a 'mystery brunette' on his lap. Perversely, Doreen, his wife, was not viewed as much of an asset at the time of his leadership campaign. As Catherine Bennett wrote in the *Guardian*, Doreen Davis was seen as an 'obscure, pitiful and in almost all respects a disappointing figure who must learn to do better'. Despite thirty years of being faithfully married and generally keeping her powder dry, she still failed in her duty to raise his profile. Whatever you do, the golden rule is never tell the truth about your husband. Doreen Davies was told to be herself but was upbraided for it when she said her husband liked films with lots of shooting and that he was always in London or on the telephone.

Some MPs just get fed up with their wives. Nigel Waterson's wife reputedly discovered she was to be divorced by reading the *News of the World*. Nigel also reputedly told his first wife he was tired of looking at her bovine features. Nearby, on the south coast, Greg Barker left his wife for the male decorator.

And the tale of Mark Oaten must alert men to the dangers of what can happen when they start losing their hair, and what not to do if it does start falling out. Firstly, try not to get involved with rent boys and then tell all to a newspaper – who could forgive Mrs Mark Oaten for a bit of a sour lemon look? Would the whole trajectory of the Lib Dems have been different if only he could have fixed himself a hair transplant? Some MPs would be wiser not to try to explain. Ron Davies MP said he went walkabout on

Clapham Common 'because his wife was depressed', an action hardly likely to cheer her up.

In actual fact there have been and, no doubt, still are plenty of long and happy political marriages. There were the Callaghans – Jim nursed and protected his wife in old age and they died in their nineties within two weeks of each other. There have been the Benns, the Healeys and the Kinnocks and more recently the Blairs. I think Cherie was quite shocked and unprepared for the way she suddenly found herself in the spotlight. If only she'd read Margaret Truman's book about the role of the American First Lady in which, according to Carol Thatcher's memoir, 'The job remains undefined, frequently misunderstood and subject to political attacks far worse in some ways than those any President has ever faced.' Although Cherie has been criticised for cashing in on her husband's success, we think she has been pretty marvellous to keep it all together; the marriage, the career, and four children including a late baby to boot.

PM's wives have behaved in markedly different ways. According to Cherie Blair's book, *The Goldfish Bowl*, the Countess of Home didn't reside at No. 10 long, but while she was there calmed her nerves by knitting. Dorothy Macmillan was keen on the garden and rushed in and out with flowers and watering cans. Later Cherie Blair wrote a book, *Speaking for Myself: The Autobiography*, about her Downing Street years, which was published pretty soon after she left. The back cover says it is charming, frank and funny – probably it is, although we couldn't face wading through it. There is only so much you can take when it comes to the Blairs. We just wished she had marched right out into the street on her first morning wearing that nightie and said hello to everyone, instead of thinking what a gaffe she'd made and slamming the door. We know what Pamela would have done . . . she would have said, 'Hang on a mo, I'll go and make you all coffee.'

Sarah Brown has said her husband is messy and noisy along with other far-fetched stuff about his making time for family, friends, and anyone else who needs him. (So this is what you do with a psychology degree.) She also said, 'Gordon went to bed and woke up thinking of the country,' but didn't mention the bloody mess he'd got us in that he was now trying to dig us out of.

We can't take anything on trust of course; the messy bit was carefully calculated to make him seem like a fallible human being, but not too fallible, and someone we could reach out to. It was messy but not too messy. Sarah upping her profile has made it more difficult for the other wives – what they say and what they wear has become important again – and what is demanded is effortless chic, which is actually never effortless. In fact, staying chic can consume your entire day.

For mistresses the advice is easy: copy Frances Stevenson, the lifetime mistress of David Lloyd George. According to John Campbell's book about their relationship, *If Love Were All*, Frances would always appear in the gallery for speeches and send LG her customary note of congratulation afterwards, which usually went like this: 'A magnificent and most powerful speech. Honestly one of the very best and most statesmanlike I have heard you make. The House was very attentive and impressed . . . You were on tip-top form.'

Although there are not many vacancies for mistresses right now, for the credit crunch has had its effect on the ability of MPs to afford 'gifts of money and little trinkets' so much appreciated by Christine Keeler. Sarah Symonds, author of *Having an Affair? A Handbook for The Other Woman*, has pointed out that mistresses are the first thing to go during a squeeze, along with private golf club membership.

MPs need to watch out if they dismiss the mistress without due notice however . . . there's something called unfair dismissal these days or, if that fails, what has come to be known as direct action. Remember Pamela Bordes, who was an ex-Miss India with a Commons pass. She was involved with a lot of movers and shakers, from Adnan Khashoggi to dear reliable Colin Moynihan. (Can this last possibly be true? Can the Internet be wrong?) They all got off scot-free it seems, except Andrew Neil. When Neil gave Bordes the heave-ho, she poured his single malt down the drain, cut up his suits and scrawled obscenities on mirrors.

Not all that many MPs have just the one wife, even if they don't all try to run their women concurrently like Alan Clark. They are starting to copy the 'European model', especially since 'having an affair is now no bar to candidacy'. Even in Catholic countries like Italy they are surprisingly forgiving and shrug off the way Berlusconi behaves. He's just a bit of a lad, and anyway he owns most of the TV stations. And President Sarkozy married Carla Bruni five months after divorcing Cecilia, who actually looked very like a slightly older Carla. Germany's Gerhard Schroeder is on wife number four, at the last count, and the German foreign minister Joschka Fischer was married five times.

Recently Carla Bruni-Sarkozy has been asked to 'lower her profile'. There was a stage when it was thought Carla was getting a bit too glamorous and camera conscious, and then she confounded everyone by stepping down from the plane looking prim and demure. She might have got a bit bored with the gadabout in any case, and she's reportedly not keen on Nicolas going for a second term.

These leaders don't like their wives to attract too much attention. JFK said on his first visit to France that he was simply the man who came to Paris with Jackie Kennedy. Leaders want their women to reflect glory on to them, not dazzle or distract the audience. This is what Mary Wilson, who was very discreet, thought about it all: 'A Prime Minister's wife is expected to be there on public occasions, to be unobtrusive at times of crisis, to be as wise as a serpent, harmless as a dove; I always tried to be the wise owl in the oak – "the more she heard the less she spoke".' Certain PM's wives, like Norma Major and Audrey Callaghan, took on board this advice, although Norma's decision to remain in the constituency rather threw wide the doors to you know who.

Now they have all been 'neutered' by the expenses scandal, how will MPs raise their profiles from now on? Sex can confer status. John Major leapt up in everyone's estimation when we heard about his affair with Edwina Curry: 'He was a gentleman and always sat in the tap end when we had baths together,' she said. She said she would have kept quiet about this had he not said he was ashamed of the affair, so not totally a gentleman after all. Quid pro quo, we think.

As is the custom with government, we have added an extra little something to this chapter to give it more weight. Rather like, 'Children, Schools & Families', we now call this chapter (or this addendum), 'Wives, Mistresses and Families', as they all seem to come under the same bracket. Note: every time a department is renamed it seems to cost between £25,000 and £176,000 of our money. Revenue and Customs were reported by *The Bumper Book* to have spent £720,000 on a different image, which in all likelihood just meant new stationary and logo.

MPs love their families (we have never had so many children at No 10, although it's a pity they can't play hoops in Downing

Street). At least they love them when suddenly more time with them is needed, either because they cocked something up and need to lie low for a while, or because they are about to be sacked, or because they need a bit of a rest while they work out their next move. These sojourns never last long; they soon get bored with the school runs and taking out the rubbish. Alan Milburn quit as Health Secretary when he'd had enough of all that blame and malarkey, but was back at Westminster strutting his stuff before you could say Jack Robinson. Michael Gove and Andrew Lansley 'flipped their homes' but said it was for the benefit of their families. Yeah, right.

It seems that what Bill Cash did (unnecessarily renting his daughter's flat, at the taxpayer's expense) was all within the rules. He has been vindicated by his local constituency association, although there is no smoke without fire. Ian Gibson (Lab. Norwich North) did something a bit similar and resigned forthwith.

Some MPs do worry about their relationships – not all sail blithely on. David Tredinnick, Tory MP for Bosworth, tried to spring the cost of a course on intimate relationships on to the electorate. His request was declined, but this was yet another interesting factoid to appear on the expenses spread sheets. Greg Barker's mobile phone bill was £7,000 in one year – an astronomical amount by anyone's standards – was this all on parliamentary business? What a chatterbox. How time-consuming it must be, maintaining a profile.

Bill Deedes wasn't at all keen on spending time with his family and according to Stephen Robinson structured his working week to see as little of Hilary and the children as possible: 'Deedes' favourite outdoor activities were scything and mowing the lawn, the latter being a particularly good means for a man to indulge in deep concentration while shutting out the world: the telephone cannot be heard and intruding family members can be warned off with a sharp yank on the throttle.'

Not that this is necessarily a bad thing. Parents are around a lot if they are out of work but this doesn't seem to help on rough estates. 'Quality time' is the thing, or was. This is a hackneyed and over-worked phrase, which at one stage morphed into a more general and even more ghastly 'family time', as if this was some special half-hour when the family would be graced with the father's presence. We all know that genuine family time consists of Dad trying to read the Sunday papers and having his head sat on by children determined to stop him.

We're pretty sure nepotism and preferment have always gone on. 'Whose son are you?' is the first question the long suffering diary secretary will ask as a reluctant job seeker hovers at the door. Since the scandal, MPs may not be allowed to employ family members and will have to swop them all about. Before long there may be a return to the old practice of, 'What will you bid for my wife?' or, 'You have my wife, but I can tell you she's quiet fierce,' even maybe, 'I'll have your lazy intern daughter if you have my nephew, but I must warn you he's very full of himself.'

The wives are in revolt though . . . Will there be a silent protest or a sit-in at the office of Sir Christopher Kelly?

If it all goes pear-shaped in the next few months at least MPs can blame it on lack of secretarial support. This might be a time for the jobless to rush their CVs into the Commons.

Although she was on hand, the wife of Nicholas Winterton couldn't stop him from slapping another female on the backside. His 'victim', Natasha Engel (Labour), said he was just an 'old man' – he was seventy-one, a dangerous age . . . often the start of disinhibitionism in men, so she knew how to retaliate. The

Two Little Princes

ex-wife of Nicholas Soames claimed that having sex with him was like 'having a wardrobe falling on you with the key still in the door'.

You can always redeem yourself as an MP though (although not with the ex-wife); Sir Nicholas Soames recently got together with Frank Field (who is not associated with wardrobes) to write a thoughtful, cross-party article on immigration.

There are plenty of political dynasties (although not many so well established as the Kennedys): the Benns come firstly to mind. Whatever your politics, Tony and Hilary have both worked tirelessly for whatever cause they happen to be championing. And Speaker Martin was at one time thought to be grooming his son to inherit his seat – although it is not very likely now. It's the same across Europe. Nicolas Sarkozy has had his hand slapped for over-promoting his son.

'Just like us', many MPs have had 'children trouble'. Mark Thatcher was lost in the Sahara. As Carol reports in her memoir, 'Mum had been on the phone to the British Embassy in Algiers. Twenty-four hours later, six days after they had first gone missing, Mark and his team were found unharmed. Unshaven and bemused by all the fuss, Mark greeted Dad rather too casually. "Hello," he said. "What are you doing here?" and said he'd like to go on and finish the rally. "Not bloody likely," Dad snapped.'

Sons of Blair and Straw have had formative problems with drink and drugs. The son of Patricia Hewitt, who always looks so long suffering and now we know why, was arrested on a drugs charge (cocaine) not long ago. His dad is Judge William Birtles, so he must have been pretty fed up about it too.

Children hang about these days, expecting to live in your London flat for free, or at low rent, and many parents will wonder how these MPs managed to get any rent from their children at all. David Taylor's daughter paid him £250 a month, which is extremely cheap by any London standard, but certainly better than nothing.

Has anybody checked if children ride about in the ministerial cars? The average age of a child on a parent's car insurance has risen from 25 to 31. Children are taking far too long to leave home; since the expenses scandal MPs have discovered what a nuisance this is. MP Peter Luff's children, who are in their twenties, live with him free of charge, i.e., supported by the taxpayer. The government has even put out a fact sheet which gives useful advice of the grandmother-sucking-eggs-sort, which reminds you not to do your grown-up children's washing and ironing.

It can work both ways of course. Children of MPs often stay as far away from Parliament as possible, presumably on the grounds that as George Bernard Shaw once said 'it is better for a parent to be a horrible warning than a good example'.

At the present moment in time, 200 MPs employ their relatives, which include 143 wives and 16 husbands, with 14 employing more than one family member, numbering nearly 1 in 10 of all the Commons' employees. According to the *Telegraph*, relations are paid higher than other Parliamentary staff and receive a larger end-of-year bonus.

Some family members hope you will find them the kind of job in which they have to do no work. One of the triggers of the expenses scandal was the discovery that Derek Conway had paid both his sons for doing nothing. It was the end of Derek's career but it did 'playboy Henry' no harm at all but everybody says he is a nice lad and a great socialite, who, if anyone is interested, is currently launching a range of fashion boots.

If there was one thing to be learnt by the expenses scandal it was the fact that MPs value their wives above all else. They simply cannot do without them – or their loyalty: 'My Tony is not a liar,' said Cherie Blair. Of course the wives' judgement is not always reliable; when Cherie was buying some flats in Bristol, one of which was for her son, she asked the help of a man who had been imprisoned several times for fraud.

To justify their pay these wives have an amazing range of job titles. A wife can be an Office Manager, a Senior Caseworker, an Executive secretary (as opposed to just secretary), a Diary Secretary (presumably the gatekeeper type), a Parliamentary Assistant or a Visits Manager. The last is presumably a new look Diary Secretary who prohibits visits from anyone young and blonde.

As Jane McLoughlin has written in *A World According to Women*, 'a wife's contribution was not unimportant to the family interests; in the promotion stakes, a man could stand or fall by his wife's domestic skills and efficiency', although, 'Corporate Man [or an MP say] would not be expected to acknowledge the part his wife played; it would make him look weak. On the other hand, his bosses held him entirely responsible if she failed to conform to his company's "standards".'

This is very much how it is at Westminster. Sandra was once the acceptable face of Michael 'something of the night' Howard and Sarah has had to become the acceptable face of Gordon Brown. Although she really over-egged the pudding at the party conference, 'My husband, my hero.' Surely no husband is a hero to his wife? Not often anyway, and certainly not for long.

Some wives simply can't hack it – as Ferdinand Mount, in his memoir *Cold Cream* points out: 'the wives of the two politicians I had worked for [Keith Joseph and Selwyn Lloyd] had both found the political grind unendurable'.

The advice to husbands is easy, just copy Denis Thatcher – his motto was 'Always present, never there'. Norma Major announced on TV that in 1991 'a massive unforeseen intrusion came into our lives', which many thought must have been Edwina Currie, but turned out to be an IRA bomb. Denis Thatcher's other advice was 'Never appear speaking on TV – this is the short cut to disaster' and 'Better keep your mouth shut and be thought a fool than open it and remove all doubt'.

Denis showed the nation the value of a steady partner, as his wife touchingly said: 'I could never have been Prime Minister for more than eleven years without Denis by my side.' And Denis enjoyed it very much too. He said, 'A vicarious political life is absolutely fascinating because you are not carrying the can.'

After writing this we're beginning to be thankful for the merciful dullness of some of our present MPs, Alistair Darling for instance. Hazel thinks he might be a tiger in bed. We may never know.

6

Shooting the Messenger

There is nothing so improves the mood of the party as
the imminent execution of a senior colleague.

Alan Clark

We shot Hans Blick first. It was he who said there were no
weapons of mass destruction. And then it all went from bad to
worse. We started shooting everybody. Not Dick Cheney and
Donald Rumsfeld though. (Even Pamela Bordes wouldn't have
got into bed with those two!) In fact, anyone attempting to
cuddle up with that administration needed their heads examining.
Tony Blair did this crime more or less on his own. He seemed to
be hearing voices in his head. He couldn't be wrong though,
could he? He was only doing what he thought was right.

Tony Blair didn't just shoot the messenger, he told the messenger
to come back with a more convincing message. Recalculate those
figures . . . recalibrate that clock . . . we need something more
believable . . . something more frightening to dish out so everyone
will roll over and say . . . *our saviour.* Thank goodness he had such
foresight, such knowledge.

Practised liars always come to believe it themselves.

The disappointing thing about the Great Expenses Scandal
(will it be mythologised like the Great Train Robbery?) was that
MPs who we liked to revere, turned out to be just like us. They

got away with whatever could be gotten away with; it was in the rules, wasn't it? The rules they'd allowed to be set nicely in place for themselves.

What with all the spin about businessmen and entrepreneurs and blue sky thinking, they had come to see themselves as a small business or even a company, and liked the idea of salaries as a package. Companies had bonuses and targets and incentive schemes so they thought they'd have a bit of the same, and that's how it all came about.

To maximise their potential, they'd dragged in family members who did a lot or a little or absolutely nothing, but somehow by dint of weight of numbers, were all on the payroll and contributed to the whole.

This all came about because of the Freedom of Information Act. What a good idea that turned out to be, although at first they tried to exempt themselves from it. One or two MPs had foreseen what would happen, but nobody took much notice of them. This was Chris Mullins's diary entry for 1 May 2002: 'Andrew Mackinlay dropped a little bombshell at this afternoon's meeting of the parliamentary committee. Apparently, under the Freedom of Information Act, by January 2005 MP's expenses will be subject to public scrutiny, retrospectively. Goodness knows what mayhem that will cause. "We are in a jam," said Robin Cook. "Few members have yet tumbled to the juggernaut heading their way." '

There had been little scams before. Remember Neil Hamilton and 'cash for questions' and the way he and Christine had to re-invent themselves as TV personalities who would do anything for a lark; or Joe Kagan and Lord Brayley buying and selling peerages, or the murky episode of Shirley Porter's (who was in charge of Westminster Council) gerrymandering? It was estimated that during the Shirley Porter scam, £21.25 million was lost, not including the £2.6 million Porter paid tenants to vacate their properties and the £2 million of extra costs for housing the homeless. She also famously sold three council cemeteries for 5p to asset strippers, who then abandoned them to vandals. 'Of course the government should do what is right, but not if it affects marginal constituencies,' said Frank Weasel (Jim Hacker's Special Advisor in BBC's *Yes, Minister*).

This new scandal just came crashing in like some horrible missile, infesting both their Houses like a plague. And every time the all-clear sounded and they came out from under their desks, those *Telegraph* journalists came out with more and more and they had to duck again. Although they couldn't use that word because it encapsulated it all, and made them look very stupid. That duck-island just can't be redacted. It comes back to haunt them like the Ghost of Christmas Past.

The scapegoat was old Michael Martin of course. Soon to be (or is already) Baron Martin of Springburn, of Port Dundas in the City of Glasgow (sounds impressive, doesn't it). His sacking was eased by the peerage, which has always been a good way to get rid of MPs. They were all trying to get shot of him in any case, as they thought him a bit of a bumbling fool and there is still quite a lot of snobbery about. At the same time, they actually all felt quite guilty about blaming him because they knew what a lot of flak they would have given him if he had done anything different. Although he resisted moves for greater accountability, they were all benefiting and that was just the way it was.

Never mind that some of it looked actually fraudulent, and that lesser mortals could be sent to gaol for what MPs had been up to. These men were quite special . . . Honourables . . . and thought it fine to give back what they hadn't really stolen, or that it was even all right to just give back some of it.

A friend of ours was encouraged by Citizen's Advice to apply for job-seeker's allowance when her husband walked out. She did this in good faith, but in a few weeks her husband sent her some money and her income rose above the government threshold. Before she could sort out her situation and money (and being in a general state of shock) she was accused of obtaining money fraudulently and summoned to a DHSS office and interviewed under caution with her testimony recorded, and to be sent on to the prosecution service. Although she had a previously un-blemished record she was obviously a soft target. We wonder what the consequence for our friend might have been had she used the words 'oversight', 'inadvertent', 'technical breach' or 'administrative error' in her defence. Or how 'scroungers' and 'benefit cheats' would fare caught red-handed with bath plugs, dog food and toilet seats?

Some time ago there was a very good Parliamentary Standards Commissioner called Elizabeth Filkin, who was considered too much of a busybody and was gotten rid of very quickly by that mysterious body: The Powers That Be. The new body to oversee standards will be made up of 'someone who has held high judicial office, an auditor and a former MP'. You could say spot the difference.

There is panic everywhere; it is very dramatic, very Shake-spearean: (*To be, or not to be, that is the question: / Whether 'tis nobler in the mind to suffer / The slings and arrows of outrageous fortune/ Or to take arms against a sea of troubles . . .*) and MPs just do not know what to do. They were all in it together though. The great thing about whistleblowers is their determination to expose all parties and all ranks.

In trying to exculpate themselves they have tried to blame Andrew Walker, the Head of the Commons' fees office, who is 'highly unlikely' to keep his job because 'his staff were found to have waved through' and 'even encouraged' questionable claims. Interestingly, Mr Walker's salary was £130,000, about twice the basic rate of an MP.

It is sure to take months to sort out. Three different men have been charged with the problem. The government likes things in threes, (three Iraq enquiries for example). First there was Sir Thomas Legg, who acted as a kind of super-accountant and told everyone to pay the money back, then there was Sir Christopher Kelly who made proposed changes to the system, and then Sir Ian Kennedy, who is in charge of implementing the changes (although he is said to be 'unhappy' with some of them, which in government speak is a euphemism for 'not at all keen'). He is chairman of the Independent Parliamentary Standards Authority and is paid £100,000 for a three-day week, presumably a salary in line with 'natural justice'. The newspapers report he is stressed in this new job and close to quitting, even though his aides say he is fully focused.

Perhaps the Parliamentary Ombudsman should be called in to help out, or is this office already overloaded with complaints from MPs who don't want to pay their expenses back? They were obviously anticipating problems as far back as last August when they advertised for a new Service Desk Assistant at the fairly, by civil service standards anyway, modest salary of £19,500 plus benefits. Not bad for what sounds like a receptionist and we now all know about those benefits. On top of all this, as if it didn't sound enough, another Sir, Sir Paul Kennedy, a former Court of Appeal judge and now the Interception of Communications Commissioner, will consider written appeals. If they don't all tie themselves in knots, Hazel and I will do it for them.

Still, it's all small beer compared to other areas of government waste. As Geoffrey Wheatcroft says in *Yo, Blair!* (supported by a mass of evidence in *The Bumper Book of Government Waste*), 'what's wrong with PFIs and PPPs is not that they are too capitalistic or free-enterprising but they are rip-offs which defraud the taxpayer'. *The Bumper Book* spells it out all too clearly and it is obvious that they live on a kind of fantasy-island when it comes to procurement (yes, that word again). Here are some factoids provided by this very useful book:

Number 10's staff budget last year came to £11.8 million.
Number 10's Press Office employs 18 civil servants and costs £1.6 million.
The amount of money the Cabinet Office spends has increased significantly over the last few years: In 2000–01, it was spending £19 million on 'supporting the Prime Minister'. This year it's spending £46 million. In 2000–01, it was spending £62 million 'supporting the cabinet'. This year it's spending £119 million.

Quentin Davies, he of bell-tower fame, has been given a right rollicking by Bernard Grey who was charged with looking into defence spending and who said: 'The MOD has plans to acquire equipment which are significantly in excess of any budget that's going to be available to them.' Presumably Quentin Davies was as equally optimistic about getting money for the military as he was claiming expenses for his own roof. The most damning bit of this report went as follows: 'It seems as though military equipment acquisition is vying in a technological race with the delivery of civilian software systems for the title of "world's most delayed technical solution".' No bonuses for this set of boffins then. Other computer systems that have been jacked-in (pardon the pun) by Jack Straw, or scaled back, include the C-NOMIS computer system which was to link prisons with probation, now it is to apply to prisons only. Also the National Identity Card programme, which nobody wanted to have in the first place, even less pay for, has been abandoned because of the credit crunch. Although in fact, the credit crunch has merely been used to avoid loss of face.

Before we started writing this book Hazel and I knew about bonuses in the city, but what we didn't know was that everyone but ourselves was paid a bonus. In our time we have been shop assistants, a cleaner, a blackcurrant picker, a chambermaid, a cocktail waitress, a painter, a designer, a teacher, a housewife, a mother, a general factotum and writers, and not once have we been paid a bonus. We'd like to go back and claim all those bonuses we should have had, which everyone was getting but us, and claim on behalf of all those others who didn't. Applying the rules liberally we could be owed a lot in fares – for instance, travelling from South to North Manchester on the bus to teach school children and then out to Macclesfield by train to take an evening class. It seems we should have billed the taxpayer for a first-class fare. As well as bonuses, civil servants in the shape of education officials (it would be interesting to view their shape after so much sitting), bought 60,000 first-class tickets between 2006 and 2009 and ran up a £10 million bill.

We had simply no idea the ridiculous amounts some people are paid. Who knew that the director-general of the BBC was paid £834,000 a year? As much as a footballer. And worse still, 46 BBC staff are paid more than the Prime Minister. Just think how many new programmes could have been made with that money if they had been paid properly, i.e. much, much less. The *Telegraph* discovered that the head of the BBC had claimed more than £1,200 in expenses before he'd even started his job. The country owes a great deal to the *Telegraph*, and other journalists.

Also we learned that 700 civil servants are between them earning more than £100 million in bonuses. We see now that instead of taking advantage of further education opportunities we should have joined GCHQ Cheltenham along with most of Julia's classmates.

Perhaps they think they are entitled to lots of money because of their very grand titles. When we had our meeting with Theresa May, her assistant 'B' (something before 'C' at MI5?), or perhaps Bee, described herself as Theresa's 'Chief of Staff' and for a minute we thought we had been magicked into the White House. The funny thing was, there didn't seem to be any other staff. Had they gone into hiding?

We suppose we can't blame civil servants from the Education Department for the state of the railways, they already have enough on their plate, but we do see why trains are not being improved if officials (along with the Queen, who was recently glimpsed catching a train to Kings Lynn) travel in a different type of compartment. Some of the peers have complained about not being able to travel first class any more and how they might have to sit in the guard's van, which shows how out of touch they have become since there are hardly any guard's vans any more and precious few guards. Anthony Trollope knew the type: 'He could not seat himself in a railway carriage without a lesson to his opposite neighbour that in all the mutual affairs of travelling, arrangement of feet, disposition of bags, and opening of windows, it would be that neighbour's duty to submit and his to exact.'

We're hopeful that now MPs will have to travel home to their constituencies instead of affording a flat in town, they will address the problems of filthy stations and late running trains, rather than just complain that these unstaffed stations are not safe for women. Here is a simple suggestion: put on station managers and security staff. Perhaps even turn NEETS from poachers to gamekeepers (keep us safe and them off the dole).

Women in the 70s 'reclaimed the streets'. Obviously this battle is still to be won. If streets are not safe at night, it is the duty of our MPs to make them so. Some have said the new rules will deter women from becoming MPs: what bunkum. Women are made of sterner stuff. If we can run the selection gauntlet we can manage to travel on the last train. If female MPs are likely to be raped, it must also apply to the rest of the population.

We fear, however, that things will slide back, rather in the way that bankers have starting dishing out bonuses again without a by-your-leave or any kind of interregnum. London MPs will find a way of avoiding late-night stations. Or there will be instigated a 'Testing the Journey Time' inspectorate, which will declare no London flat if the commute can be done in under the hour. MPs will bleat that this is not fair, 'the train was on time that day but that's not normal', etc. Perhaps the inspectors will be allowed to spot check the journey time over a six month period and only on aggregate will they know if they qualify for an allowance or not. MP David Gauke has already piped up that his journey time is usually doubled by train delays. Anyway, it can all be put on a flow chart and somebody can knock up a computer programme to make the calculations more complicated and the spread-sheets more impressive. Which will tell them the usual: not much.

Not that this journey-time inspector will last long. Regulators never do. They always feel stressed and upset because everyone is against them. Dr Ken Boston was head of the QCA (don't ask us what this stands for) for a short time but resigned after the SAT's disaster. In fact that is what regulators seem to be for, to be shot at. Electricity companies are furious with Ofgem right now and are 'doubtful about further investment'. Alistair Buchanan, Ofgem's chairman, has said he will throw the book at them if customers' bills do not fall. We wish we could believe any of this; he could have thrown the book this year if he were serious.

Ofcom (they are all called Of-something) have tried to get cold-calling companies to reduce their number of silent calls, but have failed. They found that 49% of customers felt much inconvenienced by them. It is a pity they did not ask how many customers were inconvenienced by telemarketing in general.

The Baby P case threw up all sorts of anomalies where inspectorates are concerned. Sharon Shoesmith was made the scapegoat and sacked (that sorted it all out nicely, nothing more to be done), yet weeks before Peter died, Haringey Council had been about to receive a good report from Ofsted, which was then hurriedly changed, various bits of information being mysteriously lost or withheld in the process.

Ofwat seems to be doing better than the rest. Perhaps Ed Balls could get 'a federation' of Ofwat regulators to band together to show how it can be done. Although he already seems to be in charge of too many departments . . . perhaps his effect should actually be watered down.

Luckily he is not in charge of the NHS, where nine Trusts rated excellent or good were actually failing patients. Hospitals seem to have too many regulators contradicting each other's findings. The Care Quality Commission is one regulator, another regulator, Monitor, is in charge of improvement, and the *Good Hospital Guide*, published by Dr Foster, rates hospitals according to safety indicators. Dr Foster recently flagged up twenty-seven Trusts with unusually high mortality rates. In 209 cases, swabs or drill bits were left behind after surgery and surgeons operated on the wrong body part eighty-two times. Is it possible, as well as difficulties with adding up, that poor language skills of some doctors and nurses may have contributed? If patients and visitors cannot always understand them, perhaps they cannot also understand each other. According to *The Bumper Book of Waste* last year the National Audit Office revealed that half of all incidents in which hospital patients had been harmed could have been avoided if lessons had been learned from previous incidents.

Regulators, like governments, tend to blame the previous lot. The Quality Care Commission is a re-brand of the Healthcare Commission (money wasted on websites and headed notepaper no doubt). Still, we were pleased to read that the QCC's visit to Basildon Hospital was unannounced, otherwise the dirty trolleys, bedsores, and blood on the floors and curtains might never have been spotted.

Perhaps rather than just reporting and putting the frighteners on everybody, Ofsted could become 'task-force-oriented' and actually show how it could be done properly?

Or might it be a good idea just to employ more teachers, nurses and cleaners. Or would that simply be too daring and risky?

Another strange thing about governments, and sometimes newspapers, is that they weigh minor scandals in much the same way as major frauds; if you have to dish the dirt on the other party anything will do as long as it's negative. Cherie Blair was once caught out, in the days when someone was gunning for her whatever she did, for charging the taxpayer the cost of her hairdresser. With her legal background, she neatly side-stepped the issue. Being a barrister was useful training as Tony Blair's wife; you always need a good defence, either that or a precautionary lobotomy.

Tessa Jowell was the next in trouble. Her husband, David Mills, had become involved in some way with Berlusconi and, like most female MPs, she was lambasted by the media for it. It seems that she agreed to re-mortgage her house for a short time to prop up one of her husband's business ventures, which might have been dodgy, or it might not. He said in a long-winded letter to the *Independent* that all she did was sign a charge over their jointly-owned house by way of guarantee for a personal loan. Anyway, it all got very sticky for poor Tessa and she was accused of not being fit to have been Minister for Women (this was past tense at the time) if she couldn't keep a better eye on her own household accounts.

Speaking from experience, we know many women who have been pressed into a re-mortgage by a belligerent husband, and if you tried to keep a beady eye on the type A man's accounts you would have no time for a career yourself. This is most aptly demonstrated by Wendy Cope's poem 'He Tells Her':

> He tells her that the earth is flat –
> He knows the facts, and that is that.
> In altercations fierce and long
> She tries her best to prove him wrong
> But he has learned to argue well
> He calls her arguments unsound
> And often asks her not to yell.
> She cannot win. He stands his ground.
> The earth goes on being round.

This type of man achieves his aims by coercing you into signing when you are tired or distracted. In fact there are many of these egotistical bullies in Parliament and we bet they can be even more pernicious and manipulative on their home patch. Attempting to stand up to them is like trying to hold off a rubbish crusher. Better not to get into bed with them in the first place, but they are adept at not displaying their Panzer-tank side during courtship, so it's easy to be lulled into a sense of security.

As it happens it's goodbye Alpha male in Westminster right now. They are all developing 'gentleman's problems'. They feel castrated by the goings on and worry about how not enjoying decent expenses (being made 'to live like church mice') will affect their ability to do their job. Alan Duncan feels especially aggrieved, 'No one who has done anything in the outside world, or is capable of doing such a thing, will ever come into This Place again the way we are going. Basically it's being nationalised, you have to live on rations and are treated like shit.' This little gem made it straight off the hallowed terrace into the daily papers. MPs would do well to heed Wendy Cope's words:

> Hostile, friendly, sober, pissed,
> Male or female – that's the rule.
> When tempted to confide, resist.
> Never trust a journalist.

Or better still take the advice of Lord Hailsham: 'A politician who enters public life may as well face the fact that the best way of not being found out is not to do anything which, if found out, will cause his ruin.'

7

Health and Efficiency

My idea of exercise is a good brisk sit.

Phyllis Diller

As guardians of our health MPs do work very hard. All parties say the NHS is safe with them, safer than with any other party. Everyone knows that any party who abandons this sacred cow won't get in next time. There are indeed very many good things about the NHS; the skill of the doctors, the fact that it is free at point of use (and freedom from this kind of worry must lead to better health); in many ways, it is the envy of the world. Bill Deedes stayed with the NHS right through his life, in fact to the bitter end, 'as a reaction to the awful memories of having to sell the family silver to pay for Julius's [his son] blood transfusions'. As all MP's wives will know, in fact all wives, and as Edgar Watson Howe once said, 'A good scare is worth more to a man than good advice.'

There are niggles, of course – certain drugs are rationed, waiting times for surgery are often too long, car parking is difficult and so on – but in general it is something we can and should be proud of. Although it is often lumbering and inefficient (which slightly contradicts what has just been written), everyone who works in the NHS and everyone in the UK wants to get it right. All our hearts are in it, which can only be a good thing.

The things that aren't so good are the low levels of staffing, certainly where nursing and midwifery are concerned, and (more contentiously) the levels of staff fitness. More than half the NHS staff are overweight and 300,000 are obese. One of us once had our BMI (just teetering on the edge of normal) read out by a slightly tutting nurse who could not have been less than 20 stone. Neither was it pleasant to have a breast examination by a fat, blubbery male doctor.

The management in so many areas is poor. There is profligate waste of money on agency staff. Not that statistics mean much in themselves, but the figure was 1.3 billion for the past two years. If the NHS cut agencies out these people would have to work for them direct if they wanted to work at all, and would be much better value for money. Also, their standard of education could be much more closely monitored.

The cleanliness of hospitals is always cause for concern. This worsened some years ago when services were out-sourced and there was nobody to call to account when things were done badly. The boss, still less the cleaner, like Macavity, was never there. Wages were poor and there was little loyalty, team spirit, or pride in the work, with listless operatives, often new to the country with hardly any English, doing the work for a pittance because it was all they could get. The fact that so many filthy hospitals still abound (it seems every week there is a scandal or other) suggests this problem has never been properly addressed.

Another important move forward should be towards preventative medicine. Unfortunately there is much kudos associated with ground-breaking new surgical techniques, but less glory in finding ways to stop illness in the first place. To be fair, some good work has been done developing vaccines, but there is still a great deal to be achieved vis-à-vis 'you are what you eat'.

Sometimes government schemes are put in place, but totally ignored. Just recently Martin Hickman, the consumer affairs correspondent of the *Independent*, ran an interesting piece about hospital food. This was more or less how it went: 1995, Albert Roux launches nutritional guidelines (you wonder why in-house dieticians are not up to this). Most hospital caterers ignore them. In 2000, a £10 million NHS plan commits to a new menu designed by chefs. In 2001 Lloyd Grossman, at more expense, fronts a Better Hospital Food Initiative which creates 300 recipes. Most hospitals ignore these. In 2003 there is a £2.5 million Public Sector Food Procurement (that procurement word again) Initiative which aims to raise consumption of healthy food. Six years later, ministers replace it with a Healthier Food Mark, whatever that might be. Then a survey in 2009 finds patients are served worse food than prisoners. Presumably they carried on ordering white bread and bags of frozen chips, just as they'd always done.

Alas, there is nothing in our research to suppose that this kind of inertia and what could be called 'ignorals' is not endemic in many areas of government business. They admit to 'systemic' failures themselves because it sounds as if it is not really their fault, and it is true that ministers do carry the can for an awful lot. While argument is going on, problems with hospital food remain. One of our mothers, eighty-five years old, following surgery for a broken hip, was told she must eat her breakfast cereal lying down because there was nobody to sit her up, and on another occasion, was given dry Weetabix with water as a meal. As well as making sure decent food is actually available, can somebody please make sure it is actually eaten?

Of course, this is anecdotal and because we are grateful to the NHS, once we are out of hospital we don't like to complain too much, but if everyone's anecdotes are spliced together they turn into statistics, which should send alarm bells ringing. Imagine what would happen if a division bell rang every time someone was served cold custard or there was an overspend on a useless, (usually computer) project. MPs would never stop running, and keep themselves very trim in the process.

Something that would have helped everyone – doctors, nurses and patients – would have been the Connecting for Health scheme. This, had it worked, would have meant whatever was wrong with you, wherever you happened to be ill, whatever locum was on duty, your records would be available. We've often marvelled at the waste of time for both patients and staff with the amount of duplication that goes on – filling out forms in not just different hospitals, but in the same hospitals, and often even in the same departments of hospitals.

This project was four years behind schedule and over budget at £12.4 billion, but nobody could get it to work. And now in the wake of the credit crunch (phew, what a relief, otherwise how were they to get out of that one, the crash came not a moment too soon), Alistair Darling has said it isn't essential. You would have thought that whoever said it could be done at an original price of £2.3 billion should be made to finish it for free. Perhaps a team of the kind of women who get things done, such as Betty Boothroyd, Ann Widdecombe, and Hazel Blears, could be mandated to oversee this? Not that it was the only computer fiasco. Two years ago the personal details of junior doctors were mistakenly released on to the web and what had supposedly been designed as a fairer system meant there was a mad scramble to get jobs, and as many as 30% would be without. Although we have a shortage of doctors in A&E, geriatrics, palliative medicine and obstetrics, none of it really made sense, and nobody, least of all the doctors themselves, could make head or tail of any of it.

There are other obvious things wrong with hospitals. Governments can't seem to decide whether hospitals should be large or small. If you look at it one way, the bigger the system the more money it soaks up, but in another way streamlining sounds so cost-effective (centres of excellence) and that makes sense too. Yet every small town wants to save its cottage hospital and its small maternity unit. People campaign to keep their user-friendly local services, where relatives can visit and parking is easy. In large hospitals, if you are a relative, it is very hard to get to see a doctor (you don't see them very often even if you are a patient), and they are almost never there during visiting hours. Sometimes you are told they might show up but he or she never does. You can hang around for days on the off-chance with no sightings at all. Sometimes a doctor does appear, but he doesn't seem to know anything more than you know or he is not the doctor actually assigned to your family member.

Sometimes you can be bedded down next to another patient

guaranteed to make you feel worse, not better. One of our relatives, Jenny, was rushed into hospital with an infection following treatment for breast cancer and put on a mixed ward next to an elderly man who shouted and raved all night. Whatever the effect of the drugs she was given, she didn't sleep a wink, so hardly helping her immune system to fight back.

Once, at Eastbourne Hospital, due to overcrowding another relative was in the wrong ward. He was 'under a doctor' somewhere, but none of the nursing staff on duty that day had ever met this doctor or even knew who he was. When asked if he could be spoken to or e-mailed or rung, or whether a message could be passed on for him to ring back, the staff were at a loss. Polite requests were met with lack of comprehension, blank stares, or a 'don't bother us' attitude. At the time he was in hospital he had an eye appointment at ophthalmology, two floors down. There was no joined-up thinking and nobody wanted to take him there or sort out this problem; in fact it was obvious they couldn't care less. One of us was supposed to be working that week but couldn't because he needed someone as a full-time advocate. Without that intervention, he would have just lain in bed.

The strange thing is that one of our sons happens to be in his first year at medical school and to be accepted for training had to jump through what seemed like a thousand hoops to test his 'fitness for purpose'. As well as academic ability, the main one seemed to be testing his communication skills and ability to make good judgements. With one or two notable exceptions, the doctors and nurses seen at Eastbourne have seriously lacked these particular skills. And we know that many other people across the country, not just here in Sussex, share our concerns.

We expect quite a number of MPs, particularly after the worry of the expenses scandal, are anxious about their own health. Men tend to be bracketed into two categories, those who in spite of being quite tubby declare themselves to have the immune system of an Olympic athlete (to the amusement of their family), and those who rush to the Internet at the onset of every minor symptom.

Still, like William Leith in his book *Bits of Me Are Falling Apart*, they are often pretty wary of visiting a doctor in case it causes financial upset: 'I can't go to the doctor about this mole because I have applied for life insurance, and I have given the insurance company permission to ask my doctor for my medical records, and if I were to consult my doctor before he received the insurance company's letter, and if he thought my mole was worth checking, and my insurance would be delayed and my premiums would be huge . . . '

At a glance MPs don't look that healthy; although it is known from their websites that they like to try to stay fit. An exercise bike was once spotted in John Prescott's house, although we have no way of knowing whether, like most such bikes, it was there for intention rather than actual use. Opposition members often look rather healthier. Although they are still climbing the pole and waiting for their moment, they are not in the direct firing line and are not so burdened by ministerial boxes.

Female MPs don't seem to be quite so unfit and with one or two exceptions are not especially fat although more than a few are quite plump and would have their BMI frowned upon. It is known that women look after their health better and we expect they burn up a lot of nervous energy just dashing about, especially if they have to do the supermarket shop between PMQs and the afternoon sitting.

We can tell from their websites that a great many MPs play

golf, or would like to play; even some women MPs, which is not surprising as it would go with the competitive territory. As a non-golfer once married to a golfer, one of us used to have to administer Nurofen to the golfing hero and once had to take him to A&E when he'd sprained his ankle on the 9th hole, so it is hard to say how healthy golf actually is. He used to come back quite grumpy sometimes so we wouldn't say it particularly diffused stress. And it had no effect on his Pickwickian shape. Still, it got him out and about in the fresh air, which was always a good thing.

Speaking of Pickwickian, quite a number of MPs have problems when it comes to their waist to height ratio. The first two to come to mind are Charles Clarke and Eric Pickles (this may be a factor in their scandal-free past). Charles Clarke was allowed to give up his ministerial car for health reasons; although perhaps only Mrs Charles Clarke knows if it made any difference. In the light of recent housing events we hope he is not in need of a mortgage or insurance policy. John Prescott, another heavyweight, according to Chris Mullin anyway, had very bad posture at work: 'His idea of conferring is to lie slumped in an armchair and deliver, at breakneck speed, a series of diatribes on whatever has hit him on the way into work.' His advisors were made to sit behind him on upright chairs, so they had straighter backs, if not, after all this was over, clearer heads.

Although we are not saying that the MPs have caused an obesity problem merely by bad example, it is true that we have all put on weight. This trend has come across the Atlantic. We remember working in the US during the 1970s and being shocked to our boots at the size of everyone. We watched in amazement as American TV ran ads for Dunkin Donuts back to back with warnings about heart disease, without anyone apparently seeing the connection. The last thing Britain wants is a special relationship with the American shape. This American shape, which is becoming our own, is memorably described by Simon Gray in his final book, *Coda*, describing the characters he encountered on the island of Crete not long before his death. We have also taken our 'look' abroad alas: ' . . . all nationalities, English, Welsh and Scottish, passed by in what frequently looked like the costumes of their countries, the Scotidge were dumpy in tartan shorts and shirts, the dumpy men in nursery jumpsuits I took to be the Welsh. The English wore a combination of the infantile and the threatening – cut-off trousers with chains looping out of the pockets and shirts that had no sleeves but were tattered at the shoulder, as if they'd been ripped in a drunken rage, although were no doubt sold that way, and were probably expensive – these were the young men, and mainly the young women, but the middle-aged and elderly were merely inelegant and dowdy, the women in unbecoming tracksuits and shapeless dresses – or – if they were fat – shorts and T-shirts with slogans on them . . . '

There is talk of GPs starting up weight loss clinics; part of the programme will involve regular texting to remind you to set off on your daily jog. Perhaps a pilot study should begin in the

Commons, maybe with Hazel Blears leading the tally-ho. Or David Cameron and Boris Johnson could get a cycle track set up across the Westminster village. Any slacking could be dealt with by the whips. We would also like to nominate Tim Loughton to be in charge of Conservative Keep Fit. He always looks so fresh and dapper in his summer linen suit, presumably due to the bracing wind in his south coast constituency.

Still, we mustn't advocate anything too punitive. It was apparently Carla Bruni who instigated President Sarkozy's fitness regime, causing a collapse. There are certain disadvantages to bagging a trophy wife. Gordon Brown was seen jogging not too long ago, but only the once. Perhaps John Prescott could lend him his exercise bike and then he could keep fit in the spare bedroom well away from the cameras.

Viewed from above (the Visitors' Gallery again), it is pretty obvious that most MPs could do with just a bit more exercise. They would do well to take William Leith's advice: 'Two hours brisk walking a day will gradually strengthen my heart, bringing my blood pressure down, so I will feel less frail and dizzy, and have less chance of keeling over with a stroke or a heart attack.' Also (although there is a tendency to discount this worry with the advent of Viagra) he writes, and he has obviously been sufficiently exercised by this subject to research it fully, 'Gerontologists think there is a link between sex hormones and the ability to store LDL cholesterol. Around the time you begin to lose your sex drive, the spiky balls can't be stored, so they bash into the walls of your arteries, causing scar tissue to form. These scars turn into plaques.' Scary or what!

Well, pretty scary to the average male MP. We know that type A men, which describes most of them, in psycho-medic-therapy-speak, enjoy fast cars (Alan Clark), seek multiple partners (Stephen

Norris, too many girlfriends to run for London mayor), and enjoy sexual deviations (we couldn't possibly say), although hopefully there will never be a government White Paper about it. Recently there was an NHS leaflet recommending solo sex aimed at teenagers, which we also hope was not a desperate initiative started in the Commons. It was very much ridiculed, so it was either a joke, or possibly the mistake of some e-tooler who meant to run off two copies and somehow ended up with 200,000.

Still we have to admit that having a lot of sex doesn't necessarily shorten your life and can, as the leaflet says, be useful exercise. Earl Jellicoe who appeared in our 'Wives and Mistresses' chapter, had a very long life. His obituary reads: 'Approaching ninety he still woke early for his morning swim and drove from Tidcombe to attend the House of Lords.' So sex can be good for you, and in Earl Jellicoe's case with the more women the better. He had eight children in total, including a daughter out of wedlock, which is also a useful warning that contraception is no bad thing.

In fact, the sexual goings on by MPs would probably be more informative to the average teenager than most sex guides. Adam Phillips in his book, *Going Sane*, wrote that teenagers, once adult, 'will discover that sexuality can be something so tenacious that people will risk their lives, their reputations and their livelihoods in their quest for satisfactions that don't often make sense to them'. It is true that sex manuals do not in general alert young people to this, so studying the goings on in the Houses of Parliament by educationalists could usefully fill the gap. Perhaps Mark Oaten's book, *Screwing Up*, should be on the curriculum.

One commentator at the time thought that wives might prefer to remain happily ignorant of their husband's lapses in order to continue with their marriage, which is probably true, but really for the wife to do the deciding. Cecil Parkinson's wife, Ann, couldn't really pretend ignorance once there was a baby in the offing, although it was what Alan Clark described as 'hesitations, blunderings, and aura of nerve-loss' surrounding the episode that caused his political career to falter.

It is obvious from previous chapters how much MPs depend on their wives to keep them steady. The latest research, for what it is worth, is that men whose wives go back to work full-time after having a family are more depressed than those who stayed at home to organise a happy social life. MPs are probably even happier when their wives help out with constituency matters as well, which is why they all self-combusted or dropped to the ground howling when they thought they'd have to sack them. There are some husbands in for the chop too, although nothing like as many. However much they are told what they do is 'equally valid', and however fancy their job titles, few seemed to have warmed to the idea of life in the wifely slipstream. Also, not many husbands (and this is a small sample, the experience of only us two) are fond of laying the table, loading the washing-machine, or picking up the dry cleaning.

The fitness and state of mind of MPs should be of upmost importance to the electorate. If MPs are taking important decisions on our behalf, they should not feel unwell as they do so. For example, it has often been thought that the Suez debacle was caused by PM Anthony Eden's poor health and state of mind at the time. Rab Butler, then Lord Privy Seal, thought he was 'surrounded by mad men'. Selwyn Lloyd wasn't coping either because his marriage was on the rocks as his wife, Bae, had just been in a bad car crash with her lover.

To cheer themselves up we know from many references that MPs are all partial to fruitcake. They are also partial to a drink or two, but listing their favourite tipples would take another book. They all look forward to this, often in the Members' Tearoom, and their diaries are peppered with references to cake: 'I trod the Pugin-patterned carpets yesterday, popping into the Members' Tearoom to get some fruitcake', 'I celebrated with fruit cake', 'We ate a huge tea at Gleneagles . . . ' etc.

Still, we can't blame them for the rise in obesity, so huge now it is called an epidemic. They could do something about it though. Put up the price of fizzy drinks and stem the rise of fast food outlets. At London Bridge station, for example, there is only one shop on the concourse that doesn't sell fast food, that exception being The Body Shop, which must be there to ameliorate the damage done to female beauty by excessive eating. Although most would agree that scented soaps will not do much for the type of ten-ton Tessie who likes to wolf down a meatball sandwich.

This sort of fatness is expensive as well as tragic. For a start, certain hospitals cannot deal with enormous people. Pregnant women have recently been turned away from Weston-super-Mare General Hospital if they have a BMI of more than 34, as the hospital cannot deal safely with the possible complications. One wonders how these very large women became pregnant in the first place, sexual attraction being another unexplained mystery. The next government must do something to stand up to the soft drinks industry, as it is not just our flab, but our teeth at stake as well.

Gordon Brown has confessed to eating a lot of late-night microwave meals, which might explain his pallid colour. Or he might have said it so the electorate would think he was one of them. You simply can't tell any more; nothing can be taken at face value. Margaret Thatcher was a wholesome, rather than an imaginative cook. She would often produce lasagne that someone else had made earlier, or whip up some scrambled eggs for Denis when he felt peckish. It was even rumoured that she could do a good roast chicken.

It is not really surprising that Gordon Brown doesn't have time to eat till late. He has tried to emulate Tony Blair's punishing schedule albeit in a style of his own. Rather than rueful grins and a lot of gliding between the tables as Tony was known to do, Gordon seems to have adopted the Ariel Sharon type of barge-past (Sharon was famous for knocking things over in restaurants) and Gordon Brown, the blunderbuss, has something of this style. He seems to like to conduct business on the move even though his shape is not right for it. He might have done better to clamp himself to his desk and direct operations from his big important office as Prime Ministers used to do. It can't have been good for his blood pressure chasing Obama around like a tiresome school-boy, and certainly not good for the health of his aides and minders.

Question: how come, with all the important work he had to do running the country, Gordon Brown found time to ring Simon Cowell about the mental state of Susan Boyle? Doesn't this actually call into question our Prime Minister's own mental state? We know Sarah says he always makes time for those who need him, but this is taking things to extremes. Not that you can ever ask about an MP's mental equilibrium, or lack of, without getting the brush off. Andrew Marr was much rebuked when he posed a question relating to Gordon's state of mind, even though Gordon's poor eyesight is not off-limits and was used by some to explain the rather messy handwritten letters he sent out to bereaved relatives who had lost sons in Afghanistan.

A lot of roaring around by MPs is fuelled by the demands of the 'can't stop for a minute' society, which is not necessarily particularly productive. They could certainly set us a better example. What they consider 'creatively frantic' isn't necessarily so; if only they could calm down and take stock (and ignore the hum of the Blackberry), they might actually find themselves making better judgements. It seems that Tony Blair's only piece of good judgement was to hang on as PM as long as possible knowing full well that Gordon was the likely successor. But whatever is said about Gordon, you have got to admire his bloody-mindedness and endurance.

We would imagine most MPs are too frightened to admit to any kind of fatigue, which would be seen as weakness, particularly in the target-driven era. Middle managers (and MPs are under the same kind of above and below kind of pressures, as well as sideways) are said to have the worst health. You can see why all those cooks ignored the government guidelines if it meant longer hours and more work. Although Gordon Brown may be at the top, in a manner of speaking, right now he is on the ropes and as John Rae once said, a man in this particular position will have 'numerous sympathisers but few friends'.

Gordon Brown is also middle-aged and this is when gloom is most likely to set in. According to yet another survey, most of us enjoy a happy beginning and end to life but there is a trough in the middle when depression hits. Having said that, we're not sure how many of us will enjoy a happy end to life unless the government puts its thinking cap on about the elderly, but we shall see what we shall see. Women go through this depression a bit earlier than men and afterwards experience 'post menopausal zest' . . . look at Hazel Blears for instance; she is always upbeat and cheery!

Still, if you are an MP who is just about to be voted out, or like so many following the expenses scandal, forced to resign, it is not surprising you are a bit down. Right now they all feel beleaguered and harried and not themselves. Perhaps they should do as

William Leith suggests and tap into their own 'personal bright side'. They are given a lump sum (currently £64,000 tax free) to cushion the blow of departure, which is a kind of redundancy payment, although most will have seen which way the wind is blowing and will have been discreetly casting about for TV work or non-executive directorships of various kinds. Or once election fever is in the air there will be a 'sudden sally'. When the going gets tough the tough get going and they will be looking to find their own inner Donald Rumsfeld, or a lot of touchy-feely creepiness, or whatever they are told by their assigned PR person the electorate in their area requires. MPs are nothing but versatile and don't mind kissing babies or dropping in to drop-in centres in a marginal constituency.

It has been said that all political careers end in failure, although Tony Blair was having none of this and planned a farewell tour that involved TV and radio slots as well as a victory parade. We don't remember any of this happening, particularly nothing on the open-top bus front, so unlike the Iraq war somebody must have talked him out of it. He resigned from Parliament altogether, but had plenty of ideas for things he could do. He planned to sort out the Middle East and perhaps become President of Europe, but none of this actually transpired.

Not all MPs are so up-beat when they depart; some are prone to melancholy. According to Ferdinand Mount, Michael Heseltine could be very morose: 'I sometimes wonder why we bother with it all. We work our guts out to get into Parliament. We climb up the greasy pole and finally here we are' – he waved his hand extravagantly at the modernist desk and the squashy sofas – 'and what have we got to look forward to at the end of it all? The order of the boot!'

A defeat on polling day is particularly humiliating. You've

worked your socks off and you have to stand on a podium and publicly be told you have failed. It can't be easy to retain your poise, although no doubt practice for later on when, if you are successful, you will be required to say one thing while thinking another.

Mrs Thatcher wasn't at all happy to be gotten rid of, although she managed a rousing farewell speech and was defiant till the end. Although we all wondered where she would go, as she once said: 'Home is where you come to when you've nothing better to do.' To politicians power and staying in power is often an end in itself, not the means to the end. 'When taken in the refreshing waters of office,' said Anthony Trollope, 'any pill can be swallowed.' Unfortunately out of office the opposite is true, politicians will hang on to power as long as they can with every nerve and sinew. As Trollope says: ' . . . look back and tell me of any Prime Minister who has become sick of his power. They become sick of the want of power when it is falling away from them, – and then they affect to disdain and put aside the thing they can no longer enjoy.'

Sometimes only dramatic rhetoric will persuade them to resign. Leo Amery used Oliver Cromwell's words to persuade Neville Chamberlain to depart: 'You have sat too long for any good you have been doing. Depart, I say, and let us have done with you. In the name of God go!' In *Yo, Blair!* Geoffrey Wheatcroft repeated the words for Tony Blair's benefit, although we don't know if Blair did resign in response to Geoffrey's book.

Trollope's PM describes what it feels like being out of office: 'What I mean is that I can go to bed, and sleep, and get up and eat my meals without missing the sound of the trumpets so much as I did at first. I remember hearing of people who lived in a mill, and couldn't sleep when the mill stopped. It was like that with me when our mill stopped at first. I got myself so used to the excitement of it, that I could hardly live without it.'

He also describes how he thought the Duchess, the PM's wife, would feel. No doubt these mixed views were shared by Cherie Blair and perhaps eventually will be by Sarah Brown: 'She had toiled and struggled, she had battled and occasionally submitted; and yet there was present to her a feeling that she had stood higher in public estimation as Lady Glencora Palliser, – whose position had been all her own and had not depended on her husband.'

Trollope's ex-PM ignores his wife, who wants him to begin lots of new projects straight away to take his mind off his loss, but (preferring to be more like Heath) 'gradually he allowed himself to open his mouth on this or that subject in the House of Lords, with a dignity which should belong to a retired Prime Minister'.

And so say all of us!

8

Lost Property

> Not a year passes in England without somebody
> disappearing. Scandals used to lend charm, or at least
> interest, to a man – now they crush him.
>
> Oscar Wilde, *An Ideal Husband*

Apart from obvious lost items like Osama bin Laden, weapons of mass destruction, and John Stonehouse (although he disobligingly showed up again), Parliament and its offices have lost a huge amount of technological information. The job of finding it again is not easy, particularly if you don't know how much data was lost the first place.

MPs will obviously have lost sleep over the credit crunch and the expenses scandal (well, the expenses scandal anyway). How many of them were up at 3 a.m. ferreting in their drawers for documentation and receipts that they never had in the first place or didn't bother keeping, desperately fishing out bills or bits of bills in the hope that what they find can pass muster?

Seemingly more sleep was lost over this issue than the decision to go to war against Iraq. So many are so full of their own importance and mindful of their 'rights' that they are challenging Sir Thomas Legg's findings and refusing to pay the money back.

More importantly, many lives have been lost looking for Bin Laden – although rumour has it he has given us the slip and now is in Yemen along with many other jihadists who have regrouped and set up new terror cells via the Internet.

Here in England we have lost much of our countryside: fields, hedgerows, birds, butterflies and bees. If the bees go, we all go. As for missing human beings, there are lost asylum seekers, escapees from prisons, foreign detainees released by mistake. Quite often because the people who lost them didn't know they had lost them until it was pointed out to them.

Data systems have become so complicated that only criminals and e-toolers know how to access them. Technology has become so tricky that nobody knows how to factor out a million other records when they are trying to deal with just one. Might as well take them all home on the train just in case, or drop the memory stick in the car park. Or post the lot to the head office in any old plain brown envelope no matter how sensitive the information. Let them see if they can find the one in a million they are looking for.

Data in the wrong hands is not only used for unscrupulous marketing, but can have consequences far more insidious than callers peddling double-glazing, new driveways or stair lifts. Once they've got your details they can steal identities and get under your skin without you ever knowing it.

Magistrates' courts make all sorts of errors: at Derby and Chesterfield in 2008 there was a one in four error rate. This can lead to false criminal records or criminals being set free to commit further crimes. And as well as errors, so much is deliberately lost or shut down. Archives are threatened, archivists not being the kind of people with political clout – and nobody has to worry about librarians. Fewer, bigger, better, means closures and amalgamations – not integration and collaboration, and access for fewer people. Let's put it all on-line and box up some of the rest . . . who looks at this old stuff anyway?

The UK fishing industries have been lost because of EU quotas. If, by mistake, the remaining fishermen catch too many of the wrong fish, they have to throw them back, even though they are already dead. How does this make sense?

On land we have lost pubs, buses, village shops and post offices; all things that were once loved and cherished. The branch lines which were once so useful would have been even more useful now our roads are so overcrowded. So many things, once they have gone, can't be put back; it is much more complicated than you think. Take wildflower meadows with one hundred different species: one year of set-aside does not an ancient flower meadow make. All that will spring up are weeds and thistles. An old bit of wasteland designated for wildlife, littered with bits of broken bottles, does not create a sanctuary. Lose a site of special scientific interest and it is gone for good.

Cathedrals: it is their fabric that is in jeopardy. English Heritage has just lost its grant to maintain the country's greatest buildings. Who will come in to make sure they are looked after? Charities, due to the profligacy of the bankers and the government, are in crisis already (charities receive a surprising part of their income from the government via the taxpayer). It is little understood, but government funding is the biggest source of income across the charity sector; we give enormous donations to charities (those we might not ever personally support) without knowing it.

So bankers (we know you like big projects) it is your moral duty to make up the shortfall. You should give to charities like multiple sclerosis and the wildlife trusts and restore our ancient buildings. Think wildlife havens not tax havens. You know you are 'worth it'. Use your own mantra. 'Just do it.'

From Cathedrals to cuckoos: as Jolyon Laycock from the West country reports in a letter to the *Independent*, 'The last time we heard a cuckoo was in 2002. Before that fateful year, on any April day, we might have expected to hear as many as six cuckoos calling to one another across the valley.' Michael McCarthy's book, *Say Goodbye to the Cuckoo*, draws attention to this void in the British countryside. It is not just the cuckoo we are in danger of losing but the yellow wagtail, the spotted flycatcher, the nightingale, the swift and the skylark.

Delius's *On hearing the first Cuckoo in Spring* will shortly mean nothing, and yet previous generations, even those who were not interested in classical music (and interest in this seems also sadly in decline), knew this piece of music and what it said about our culture and heritage.

We have fifty-eight species of native butterfly and many of these are threatened. Children today would be thought mad to go out with a butterfly net – the numbers of butterflies are now so small. Fortunately, gardeners with butterfly-loving plants are managing to maintain populations of our favourites – Peacocks, Red Admirals and Brimstones, but nothing can be taken for granted. We must all be vigilant.

Supporting things that once looked wasteful and expensive – like cycle-paths – seems both desirable and economical now in the light of carbon footprints. It is dreadful to witness those with political power making uncaring decisions about the English countryside. Big business has always been bad for the environment. Look at GM foods for example; the British people said no to GM foods but successive governments have been lobbied by conglomerates and have bullied us into acceptance.

We have lost the night sky: light pollution has become a modern scourge. What is the problem with that? you may well ask. Well, gentle grumblings about light pollution have now become rallying cries. Dark-sky campaigners work tirelessly to protect the universe and crucially, to help conserve energy, protect wildlife and to 'rediscover the human rhythm'. The impact of the vanishing night on plants and animal was recorded as early as 1897: '[insects] are slain by thousands at each light every warm summer evening' and the report went on to say, 'when England is lighted from one end to the other with electricity the songbirds will die out from the failure of their food supply'.

MPs could do with a spot of 'stargazing'. If they became more aware of the environment, they might be more inclined to try and save it. We hope Westminster has low-energy light bulbs installed everywhere to set an example to the rest of the country.

We would like to see the next government clean up the rivers and ask why, in spite of the winter rain, they flow so slowly? It is blatantly obvious that Industry and overpopulation is demanding too much extraction. We need the kingfisher back and the otter and the water vole. Only when these can breed happily again will balance be restored. These are not 'fringe benefits'. They are our natural right. Sometimes nature has swung out of kilter on its own, it *can* make mistakes too. Here in Sussex there are too many magpies; could the government organise a cull to save the songbirds?

What has been taken away from us, in spite of supposedly greater democratic freedoms, is the right to complain effectively. There are all sorts of complaining channels (the whole of the UK has become one giant suggestion box), but these channels end in more channels and more call centres and you can't even put your complaint in writing, as there is no one to write to any more. No one has a name, or one they'd be prepared to acknowledge.

Human rights (as far as complaining goes) are all on the side of the organisation and not the complainant. And the fewer ways there are to complain, the more we find we need to.

When we became 'customers' (the customer is always right) it made no difference. Well the customer is not right any more, it seems.

Whatever the organisation, you have to fight in order to access it, especially if you are not an e-tooler or a technocrat (although we have established they don't know as much as they think or for some reason do not have the marvellous communication skills to transfer their information without losing much of it).

If you have to ring BT for instance, it is always something you have to brace for. How long will you wait – will it be circuitous – will it be complicated? Will you be lucky enough to speak to a real person? And will he or she know anything if you do? Are you in for the long haul? Will you have to give up and try another time?

Some bad things *have* been lost. Swine flu seems to be one of them (although not before one of our daughters brought it back from Val de Lobo and gave it to us all); it petered out instead of mutating into something nastier. The government acted decisively, even though Tami-flu had some strange side effects and turned out not to be as effective as was once thought. And now we have huge stocks of a vaccine that nobody needs and lots of countries including our own are trying to un-order it from pharmaceutical companies, who they are now accusing of ex-aggerating the flu risk to make money.

Not that governments could really tell who, or how many, actually had the flu. Nobody in our families went to the doctor as it said 'go away and ring a help-line' on the surgery door, or words to that effect.

Still, it means the health officials can now concentrate on the problem of binge-drinking. Unfortunately both parties are nervous of putting up the cost of alcohol before an election, although all

say they want to. The price of alcohol is at a relative all-time low and contributes significantly to this big social problem. Short-term-ism strikes again, as does a lack of joined-up thinking. Stay in power at all costs. Never mind the drunks on the streets, in A&E, and liver transplants at £1,000 a time, we can't upset the alcohol lobby and we need the tax revenue.

Another organisation we have lost trust in is the BBC. Far from being too controversial, it is predominantly bland and lily-livered. New programmes only seem to be thought provoking when the BBC wants to up their ratings, for example when the BBC let it be known that the leader of the British National Party would be on *Question Time.*

Most of the programming is dull and repetitious, particularly the local news programmes in which much of the content couldn't even be described as news. It is very middle of the road, well not really middle, quite near to the bottom.

The BBC seems to have a general fear of mentioning Israel, or mosques, or children in asylum centres, or women's issues, or anything remotely 'difficult'. Report facts – don't dare discuss or criticise governments, or offer different viewpoints. Nobody should be upset in any way. Sex doesn't matter though, it's fine to offer plenty of that, in fact everything is OK as long as you can have a good laugh and it's better to stick to a tried and tested format.

The one thing not standardised was the astronomic salary of Jonathan Ross.

We're sticking our necks out but the only decent and worthwhile news and discussion programmes occur on Channel 4 – it should have the licence fee, not the BBC.

There is one important thing that the government has lost – and doesn't even know it has lost – which is the power of silence. Ian Duncan Smith was ridiculed for his stance as a silent man and he tried to make a virtue of what he himself thought to be his own failing. But he was on to something interesting. We are not talking about strategic silences when no statement is made because the government hasn't a clue what to do. We are advocating the discipline of silent thought – the strength one can gain from mindful meditation which Anthony (the founder of monastic tradition and the first of the Desert Fathers) recorded: 'his mind was calm and he maintained a well-balanced attitude in all things'. Perhaps a 'quiet zone' should be set aside at Westminster for busy MPs to achieve clarity of thought – an essential ingredient for good decision-making.

Sitting and thinking is not considered the thing for men of action. And let's face it; MPs see themselves as men of action. But what is at stake is the ability to hold the centre, to stay calm and when necessary, immovable.

Life has so speeded up that everything harries and hectors – car alarms, police sirens, mobile phones – life is just one series of bells and bleeps. Doug Meredith, in a Remembrance Day letter to the *Guardian* noted wryly: 'It must be a sign of our times that I was asked to observe two minutes' silence at my local library.' MPs should tap into the power of silence. Silent protests are extremely powerful and make a stronger, longer-lasting statement than pushing and shoving. Remember Jesus at his trial: 'He was silent and gave no answer.'

As we have observed, MPs, like bankers and many businessmen, keep their demons at bay with frenzied and pointless activity.

We'd like to see MPs off on silent retreats, not 'fact-finding missions' with a round of golf conveniently tagged on at the end. The government should not ratchet-up the hysteria which is everywhere: it should take the lead and calm everything down. Perhaps troubled adolescents could be sent on silent training to retreats (not solitary confinement which is a very different thing) and be encouraged to look around them. In the same way that a fall of snow transforms everything, they could be transformed. Even snow, a quintessentially silent experience that we are lucky to enjoy most winters, might well be lost to global warming, unless we learn lessons and act fast.

Getting the balance right is the critical thing. Winston Churchill balanced days spent in feverish activity (and in wartime he had the excuse that there was no time to lose) with days when he didn't appear to do very much except cogitate and give out inspirational pronouncements. Sometimes these seemed merely instinctual, although one shouldn't say merely, as instinct is a very important thing. MPs overrule instinct, and the rhythm of the natural world, at their peril.

9

Not Fit for Purpose

'We're all f—ed. I'm f—ed. You're f—ed. The
whole department's f—ed. It's been the biggest
cock-up ever and we're all completely f—ed.'

Sir Richard Mottram, former Permanent Secretary at the
Department for Transport, Local Government
and the Regions

Governments always blame the previous incumbents for everything and love the word 'dysfunctional'. We shall all have to
brace for a lot of dysfunction and a lot of blaming after the next
election, whoever gets in. The Conservatives will blame Blair and
Brown, while Brown will blame Blair, bankers, America, Alistair
Darling, Ed Balls, the party and anyone else who dares to loom
into view. If only Gordon Brown had clamped himself to his
desk and just got on with it from his big important office like
Prime Ministers used to.

He can't blame his wife Sarah though, she has twittered on
valiantly, whatever the weather. This all-out blame game is
wearisome for the electorate; it's a bit like the occasional pitiful
swiping by *Guardian* and *Telegraph* readers against each other.
David Miliband, arguing with Eric Pickles, said the opposition
made him sick; it is all very schoolboy-ish. We'd prefer governments gave the sarcasm and venom a miss and used this misspent

energy to get on with the difficult task in hand. And not just set up a lot of working parties which are known to prevaricate, postpone or soothe. Or introduce more 'training'. As Quentin Letts says, this is 'today's all-purpose political get-out'; 'it creates jobs in the sector which is attacking you and it provides a line of argument to see off critics elsewhere'.

Especially as so many areas of government are, as John Reid said, 'Not fit for purpose'. Not all ministers are great speakers but the honest ones do their best to explain things. Bob Ainsworth memorably said on BBC news on 13 December 2009 that 'money is a bit tighter than it was' and saw the need to tell us that the kit needed for the army in Afghanistan doesn't come from Marks & Spencer and has to be ordered through a complex procurement process. Rather missing the point that it would be his job to make this process simpler and a lot more like ordering in from M&S. Still, having researched the procurement procedures for many departments, we can see why he was so exasperated.

Like Bob Ainsworth, a great many MPs needed help with speech writing. Ferdinand Mount was charged with helping Mrs Thatcher and this was how it went: ' . . . it is hard to convey the full horror of those speech-writing sessions. They would start towards the end of July, though the conference was not till the second week of October, and they would last for anything up to three or four hours. The first draft I served up was simply there to be torn apart and binned, while she began to think what she might actually want to say. At this stage, various characters would flit in and out of the meetings, offering a page or two, perhaps no more than a paragraph. Alfred Sherman would last only a session or two before denouncing the proposed text as trivial and banal and annoying Mrs Thatcher so much that he was told not to come back.'

Chris Mullin was also deeply contemptuous of the speeches he was given to read and invariably rewrote his own, 'The speech that has been drafted for me is so dire that I dare not read it out. It comes accompanied by a thick yellow folder containing briefings covering just about every eventuality except the possibility that I might be talking to intelligent human beings who would prefer not to be addressed by an android.'

We worry that written English may be not be safe with either of the main parties. At the Conservative Conference, delegates were asked to vote for their winning sound bite of choice between 'Cam Can', 'Yes We Cam' or 'Vote Blue not Brown'. We don't think their ideas people are quite at the top of their game.

Still, John Prescott takes the biscuit for mashing up the language. We think this directive may be something to do with our troops in Afghanistan: 'The objectives remain the same and indeed that has been made clear by the Prime Minister in a speech yesterday that the objectives are clear and the one about the removal of the Taliban is not something we have as a clear objective to implement but it is possible a consequence that will flow from the Taliban clearly giving protection to Bin Laden and the UN resolution made it absolutely clear that anyone that finds them in that position declares them self an enemy and that clearly is a matter for these objectives.'

All this on top of a Prime Minister with no military experience sending off the army 'in a poor state of preparedness'. We learnt that the MOD had 87,000 staff for 175,000 servicemen so it's not just numbers but ratios that are the problem. We know that maths is not taught well in schools because you can't find maths teachers. So down the line (or 'chain of command') this is what happens. 'Only connect' said E. M. Forster. Still perhaps it is just as well we (or even they) don't know all the statistics. The Iraq war was said to have cost £8.4 billion. We don't think they would have under-estimated; they never did with their expenses. Anyway, it's not just the MOD that can't get things right. Remember the New Year train fiasco of 2008? The work on the points so over ran that the lines were shut well into the New Year. Worse, Network Rail's contractors could not be penalised for a failure to provide sufficient staff to complete the engineering work, even though it had been established before the work began that staffing levels were critical to finishing the work on time. The rail companies tried to explain it away but it was all too obvious that it was just backside covering, and in any case, we have now become a country distrustful of even the most basic information like train times or the best way to get somewhere. We are also dished out information we can't possible need or want. Our local council, Wealden District, has sent out a full colour leaflet 'Waste Matters' about recycling, telling us to 'reuse scrap paper and old envelopes for notes and lists' and 'throw away less food'.

As we write, we are in the middle of the biggest freeze up for years and the country has slid to a standstill. There is not enough grit because councils presumably lost money during the crunch (too much dealing with Kaupthing and Landsbanki?), yet nobody has thought how much this is costing the NHS with all the extra broken limbs and the cost to businesses, who have no customers and are losing millions of pounds every minute. But councils have to work within their budget. Some councils are very annoyed as those that had stored plenty of grit have been told to give to councils who didn't bother, so there will be a lot of squabbling about who owes what to whom when the snow melts. There is a parallel here between snow, grit and middle-class pensioners. Pensioners with assets are forced to sell their homes while those who have never saved have their care home bills picked up by the state.

In all this bad weather the trains have stopped again. Not that they were that great before. We haven't sat on a clean train once this year and there is a new diktat from somewhere on high (not changing the parameters or anything) that says a train is only overcrowded if it is carrying 130 passengers for every 100 seats and punctual can now include trains that are up to ten minutes late. Rather like one of our daughters' GCSE exam when any mark over 75 meant you got 100%. Numbers are funny things. Also words: what's in a name anyway? Hire purchase was validated by the use of the credit card, sanctioning debt in the process. 'Time and motion' turned into 'studies in productivity' and 'efficiency savings'. 'Living wage' turned into 'minimum wage', although nobody knew what the first meant and the second was never enough.

There is now one surveillance camera for every fourteen of us. Yet very few crimes are solved using these cameras (supposedly one crime for every 1,000 cameras), but you wonder how they actually know this, or know anything in fact. One of us had a purse stolen on Victoria station one day, by a girl gang of thieves. There were plenty of cameras, even a team of 'watchers' in the control room, and the theft took place in broad daylight, but nobody noticed. Afterwards we thought the operators in front of the TV monitors would have been better value if they'd been walking up and down on the actual station, like Bobbies on the beat, instead of chatting away behind the scenes. You can see why cameras are not that useful; the film is grainy, someone has forgotten to put a new one in, or it took 300 man-hours of detective work to find the right bit and then you couldn't be sure it was the robbers, as they were all wearing hoods.

One unusual feature of government that doesn't happen in other organisations (or possibly ever happen, except in graduate-traineeships) is the 'cabinet reshuffle'. As Mel Wild wrote in a letter to the *Independent,* 'No business would move the director of training to be the finance director; or the overseas director to be the security director.' A reshuffle seems to be an action of last resort. Changes in cabinet are usually heralded by cries of 'completely without foundation', or 'garbage', yet this is how we know for certain a sacking or a high profile resignation is about to happen. Prime Ministers seem to think that by reshuffling the pack or rejigging either poor performers or those whose profile is too high, and thereby undermining their own position, the public will be appeased or impressed. In 1962, Harold Macmillan, presiding over a faltering government, sacked a third of his cabinet, an action to be known ever after as 'The Night of the Long Knives'.

Reshuffles are not always greeted with enthusiasm, not even by those being promoted. Bill Deedes was once rewarded with the position of 'Parliamentary Secretary of Housing and Local Government'. Unfortunately as his biographer, Stephen Robinson, says, he fretted that he lacked what he called 'the intellectual equipment' to be a minister and 'knew enough about junior government to understand this would be hard, unglamorous work and he was extremely unkeen'.

Still at least Deedes did have some aptitude for his next position. Often MPs are simply thrown in at the deep end and are supposed to master complicated briefs of which they have no knowledge or affinity. A few years later, after a stint returning to the back benches, Deedes was promoted to the cabinet proper as 'Minister for Information', a job to which he was much better suited. Nevertheless his assistant, who worked for the civil service, 'found himself in the awkward position of being unable to brief his minister on any aspect of his job' and had 'to think quite hard what the department was for'.

(By contrast, when Chris Mullin is promoted to minister it is obvious that his assistant, Jessica, could easily do his job for him and is not going to be indulgent. 'At 9.30 Jessica rang to ask when I was coming in. There was a definite tone of disapproval in her voice. I explained about the flood, but her tone suggested it was no excuse.' Later she tells him, 'Nick Raynsford worked much harder than you do.')

The long knives reshuffle had been part justified by the fact that Macmillan thought that 'younger men would look vigorous and dynamic on television'. This is something still taken to heart by modern day MPs. They all seem to like walk-on parts. Boris Johnson has been seen starring in *EastEnders* and Tim Loughton, the Conservative MP for Worthing, has recently appeared in a Channel 4 documentary dipping into life on a rough estate.

Governments try their best but everything they attempt to do has become too complicated and too in thrall to technology that it never seems to work properly. The council tax benefit take-up rate was just 65% in 2006 and for working tax credits it was just 80%. Perhaps this is why they make it so complicated to access, to appear to be dishing it out whilst keeping money in the coffers. It is no wonder that single parents (usually women) are reluctant to swop the uncertainty of part-time or seasonal work for the certainty of social security. It may not be much, but at least it's regular. Systems can't deal with sudden changes; try renegotiating your housing benefit or your job-seeker's allowance if you suddenly find yourself out of work. On the TV programme *Benefit Buster*, claimants were found work but it never seemed to last. Their managers 'collected' because they'd hit their 'targets', but there seemed no way of tracking their clients long term to see if their lives had actually improved.

Although it might seem strange to make this comparison, you can see why Afghan women might not want to change their allegiances away from the Taliban to outside forces that come and go – to a corrupt police force, or a fickle new army, still less a force of occupation which now you see and then you don't. At least the war lords protect their women in purdah. Of course they will need education, but without security this means nothing.

Here in Britain we have many dispossessed souls. In some, particularly inner city areas, the schools are poor, and the social services inadequate and fully stretched (we have seen how they deal with old people and it is not good). Staff are difficult to recruit and more difficult to keep. High staff turnover is like having no staff at all, particularly as far as the social services are concerned. How can a child build a relationship with anyone who disappears after a few weeks? And how easy it must be for a neglectful parent to play one social worker off against another. The kind of low calibre recruits available in these very poor areas are not likely to have the ability to turn anyone's life around. Sometimes the carers scarcely have higher intelligence than some of the disadvantaged mothers. In the Baby Peter case it is easy to understand how gullible social workers were deceived, although hard to forgive a paediatrician who had not noticed the child's back was broken.

But it is never straightforward. Ferdinand Mount recorded a conversation he shared with Keith Joseph, who was Education Minister in Maggie Thatcher's era: 'I said, in my best pompous Thatcherite manner, that we could not duck the subject of education, it was a central part of restoring self-discipline to society. "Ah yes," said Keith, "but schools are not the whole answer, there are these lumpen families, these terrible stories of baby battering." '

Every time there is a scandal, instead of a redoubling of efforts there seems to be a flight of fear; paediatricians are afraid to intervene, the police feel like washing their hands, agencies are told to work together, but instead there seems to be a mass retreat. When all is said and done we must not forget that it was the child's mother, her boyfriend and her lodger who caused Baby P's death, and ultimately it is they who are culpable. They were united in their depravity and sometimes all the care and the observation in the world cannot stop this happening. It has been reported in the press that Baby P's father is now suing Haringey Council for failing to protect his son. Without knowing the ins and outs of this, you must wonder where the father was, what kind of a man he was and why he allowed this terrible tragedy to happen to his own child.

It will take a great deal of government effort to make every child a wanted child or to get certain sub-groups to use contraception. How much easier can you make it to get hold of condoms? A condom is a very well designed piece of equipment immensely fit for purpose.

Political parties have to tread very carefully when they try to moralise. The Conservative Party's description of Dewsbury Moor, Shannon Matthews' estate, as drug- and crime-ridden infuriated the inhabitants who didn't see themselves that way and had banded together as a community to call for Shannon's safe return. They all felt that given their start in life they were doing their best. Not all were out of work or totally dependent on the state, nor were all of them demoralised by their surroundings.

What there were, however, were a lot of single mothers, and obviously not enough condom-wearing men. All too often a boy fathers a child and then slopes off just before or just after the birth. In this tomcat society, the toms are outside scrapping in the dark while mum and gran are inside rocking the baby. It has now become the norm for babies to be brought up by three women, mum, gran and great-gran, with hardly a male in sight. Sometimes these males do not simply disappear but are summarily dispensed with as they have nothing to bring to the party. We do worry that as society fragments, women seem to be further infantilising men. There seem to be too many boy-men hiding behind mum's skirts, or the kind of men who think if they can't automatically be boss they won't bother to play the game at all.

And so the cycle repeats itself; without fathers, these boy-babies grow up wild and uncivilised, have little self-control and are unable to get up every day to do a job even if they can find one. Sociologists say that teenage boys create gangs 'to assuage their father-hunger'.

Iain Duncan Smith's report reiterating the importance of early intervention got it absolutely right. Whichever party gets in next time we hope they will continue to support the Centre for Social Justice.

Of course, making decisions about benefits and entitlements would be a lot easier if there was some shared moral code, but because society is so ghettoised between rich and poor, common denominators are hard to find. A recent Rowntree report discovered that poor people were disliked as much as bankers. It seems to be generally thought that low earners are not doing enough to help themselves.

It is true that the underclass, as they have come to be known, have poorer health, take a disproportionate amount from the NHS, as well as absorb more police time (the worst crime is suffered by the poorest people). Also the police and housing departments deal with the same rogues and troublesome families time and time again.

Lembit Opik with condoms

Education, even with Ed Balls bouncing about with strategies, threats and sound-bites, is in stasis. Bullying teachers and imposing targets has demoralised staff rather than revived them. Recruitment is very difficult. Certain cast-offs from the Westminster village have come to the aid of schools, though. Damian McBride, who was implicated in a Labour smear campaign, was last heard of applying for a job at his old school, and Jo Moore, who was forced to resign after describing 11 September 2001 as 'a good day to bury bad news', is retraining as a primary school teacher. There are not lots of marvellous teachers out there waiting to step up to the plate. Even top schools have difficulty recruiting maths and science teachers. Attracting maths graduates with a 'we'll pay off your loan' sweetener will not work as they'll do their stint and then take the money and run. Run straight back to the city where the bonus culture is already creeping back and they can earn ten times in one year what they'd earn in a 'bog-standard' comprehensive. And it will create resentment from arts graduates who devise plays, run clubs and contribute more to general school life, but have to pay off their own student loans.

Whichever way you look at it, it is not good news for poor children. What the grammar schools had was moral authority and in many families with little ambition, they managed to subvert the mantra that to be educated was getting above yourself and rising above your station. Getting your children educated is no longer a given; it involves huge parental input. In fact, if you have several children it is practically a job in itself. New Labour has castigated mothers for falsifying addresses or moving into good catchment areas. They say this is unfair, whereas the only thing that is really unfair, is the inadequate provision of good schools.

Whatever the government says the one thing you can never really make up for is a lost education. Miss out on certain building-blocks at a critical stage and your brain remains untrained. There needs to be strength of will to tackle the deep-rooted problems, not just tinker round the edge. Margaret Thatcher, quite early on in her tenure, said, 'We must do something about education', but whoever has been in power, it has never been enough. Ed Balls' latest idea is that everyone should have the chance to learn Mandarin. We think we know what Mrs Thatcher or Keith Joseph would have thought of that. This is just a few years after the Labour government said languages should be optional. Maybe it would be better to make sure the country can adequately converse in English first.

There are plenty of things that can be done though. Deal with the problem of school refusers. Send the police in to round up truants and bring back the truant officer himself. That's something useful those Community Support Officers could do; they've never really managed to carve out much of a role for themselves except a lot of hanging about waiting to call in a trained police officer. Lengthen the school day to include art, drama and sport. Every school a green school; bring back gardening and horticulture. These subjects often transcend academic ability and can be taught to everyone at some useful level. You can't expect young people to be self-reliant if they have no skills. Politicians are always banging on about a 'skills shortage'; well, most of these 'skills', like carpentry and plumbing, can be delivered in schools without much adaptation. You don't need a flagship academy; a lick of paint and some simple equipment will do the trick. Activity is the thing. Activity is infectious and leads to achievement and then the whole thing becomes self-propelling; everyone wants to join in. Catch it while you can.

At the same time, it is vital to dispense with the shibboleth that everyone can be educated to the same standard. More modest ambitions should be held for some. Dishing out degrees to all has devalued them and employers do not know what is what any more. Jenny Diski in her book *The Sixties*, describes a family she was once involved with who were 'completely baffled by life': 'There was an almost new fridge without a door rusting in the garden. Mrs B had got it from social services, but just afterwards she heard about a newspaper report of a child who had climbed into a fridge and suffocated, because the door had locked behind him and there was no way of opening it from the inside. Mrs B, in a moment of concerned parenthood, had taken the door off the fridge. When it turned out that the fridge no longer worked (because without a door it was no longer a fridge), she chucked it into the garden.'

Once, one of us employed a couple of bouncers for a teenage party and tried to explain what they were to do (with torches, guide the cars parking in the next-door field). 'Wotyer mean? We wasn't told we ain't got to do nuffink.' The main man was only interested in telling me that 'no one disrespects him', while the other watched the boxing on TV. It goes without saying, although the fierce one was posted at the bottom of the stairs, it was the hostess who found the couples in the spare bedroom. The other one wasn't 'bovvered'; he couldn't be torn away from the telly.

Still, we mustn't throw in the towel; everyone, however hard they are to educate, need more of it, or even just a bit more of it. Respect would be a lot more common if you could actually assume some basic level of attainment. Plumbers would be greatly respected if they turned up on time and didn't complain about getting wet. Roofers the same; it would be great if they arrived at the time originally fixed, or called you if they were held up. There is no excuse for not calling, especially as when they are on site they are always on their mobiles ringing somebody. Tradesmen who could communicate properly would find everyone was much nicer to them and they would find their own lives made easier.

MPs seem to have undertaken a great deal of renovation of their second homes so none of this should be news to them, although if you are spending taxpayers' money and not your own perhaps it doesn't matter so much.

The health and beauty industry has mopped up the less well educated women so they seem less of a problem.

It is not easy even for more able pupils. They may all get A's but it's hard graft. Charles Moore has pointed out in the *Telegraph* that much of the education meted out today 'pulls off the incredible double of being very hard but very low quality. There are endless projects and modules and endless ways of remarking to up-grade one's results but no definite test of what is known and understood.' He is correct that after fourteen years of education the majority have not learnt the 'what', the 'how to' or the 'why'. In this essay he asks how many can draft a letter or e-mail, unaided, which coherently makes an argument? We would shorten that to how many can even draft a letter? And this also applies to the well educated, not just the NEETS.

So, yes, teachers have their work cut out. And Rome was not built in a day. But no more time should be lost.

10

Tub Thumping (advice for the next team in to bat)

We trained hard; but it seems that every time that we were beginning to form into a team we would be reorganised. I was to learn later in life that we tend to meet any new situation by reorganising, and a wonderful method it can be for creating the illusion of progress while producing confusion, inefficiency and demoralisation.

Titus Petronius

On the day of the pre-budget report the House of Commons was a hive of activity; there were debates and readings and committees and bills to-ing and fro-ing. And yes, the boys in the backrooms seemed to be working pretty hard as well.

What we discovered on our journey is that MPs in general work very hard, which was why they felt so apoplectic and wrongly maligned over the expenses scandal, practically choking on their ministerial cornflakes.

Frenetic does not necessarily mean productive though and the big unanswered question remains: how much of this activity, mostly carried out in good faith, is actually contributing to the Common Good? Or do meetings just lead to other meetings and to ever more papers that are either never implemented or totally ignored.

Boris Johnson is right; we do need to 'get rid of all the non-sense'. We love Boris Johnson, even though he ignored us, and even though we discovered that his own department was silted up with jargon and red tape. It is not widely known that Boris was once mistaken for John Major and we are sure that they (John and Boris that is) would both agree with John Major's assertion that 'a sound bite never buttered a parsnip'. For all our love of Boris, we do think he should start putting his own house in order first, please.

About the nonsense and being serious, we believe we are on a tipping point. If our freedoms are further removed in the name of human rights then we may never get them back. There has been an extremely worrying assault on our civil liberties, which has been brought about under the bracket 'fear of terrorism', with the emphasis being on the word 'fear'.

Could the government put 'mergers' on hold for a while as well? The Equality and Human Rights Commission was merged from 'racial equality', 'sex discrimination' and 'disability rights'. No wonder there was trouble and muck-up; people were fired and then taken on again. It was money for old rope (and worse, Andreas Whittam Smith discovered that Vera Baird, Solicitor General, tried to get the taxpayer to foot a £286 bill for her Christmas tree).

Let's get back to KISS (Keep It Simple Silly). The first job of the incoming government should be to cut out everything it can. It should take shears and scythes, to every department. Out, out, out. And once they've trimmed the red tape, cut the spin, and pared down the jargon, they should put back a lot of things that have been lost.

Things such as hedgerows, wild flowers, eagles, spotted fly-catchers, cuckoos, otters and dormice; nature walks, parenting skills, cookery and sewing, cycle paths, local railways, tram lines and grammar schools (forbidden word) or at least grammar school streams. And then they should clean up the waterways and the beaches. Why not get the NEETS to do work for welfare, or give them nice uniforms and get them away from daytime TV to plant trees and get those prisoners out to do community pay-back instead of festering in the dark. And teach the prisoners to read and write so that if they are ever back in the community permanently, they have a better chance of surviving. Fresh air, in all senses of the word, is good for everybody.

The middle classes should be mobilised as well. Fetch those gap year students to teach reading and writing in deprived areas of their own country and in exchange offset some of their rapidly rising university fees. They will learn as much from working in an inner city school, which could just be blocks from their own house, as they would in Ruanda, Botswana or Vietnam. We should all be reminded that contraception is not just a good thing, but a green issue. And instead of extending shopping hours and creating more bank holidays, perhaps the government should bring in a weekend of silence where everything shuts down for two days a year. Switch the treadmill to pause and let people see if they can cope. If they can't, then something has gone badly wrong. On the day before The Weekend of Silence, we propose that Tony and Cherie could personally re-boot Britain's economy by spending a sizeable chunk of the money they earned during their years in power. It is the least they can do. As Mrs Cheveley says in Oscar Wilde's *An Ideal Husband,* 'Even you are not rich enough, Sir Robert, to buy back your past. No man is.' But at least Tony and Cherie could try.

We wish Nicholas Ridley could buy back and put back. He was a local MP when we were growing up and we were pleased to see that he had been singled out by Quentin Letts for his book, *50 People Who Buggered Up Britain*. Ridley was responsible for allowing the Okehampton bypass to be cut through a national park and allowing wide-scale but very low-grade housing development to ruin the Gloucestershire countryside, although he opposed development at the bottom of his own back garden. Ridley also paved the way for out-of-town supermarkets, and later the

Jack Straw with Boris Johnson

shopping mall, which as Sara Maitland in her book, *A Book of Silence*, has rightly observed 'are more or less designed to be noise boxes' and which have contributed to the demise of the high street. As Norman Mailer once said, 'Conservatives are people who look at a tree and feel instinctively that it is more beautiful than anything they can name. But when it comes to defending that tree against a highway, they will go for the highway.'

Sometimes it can work the other way. When Alec Douglas-Home was made PM, post the 1963 Profumo scandal, his great advantage was that he lacked so many of the usual egotistical political attributes. We suspect this is why Angela Merkel, the German Chancellor, has been given a second term. And why Herman Van Rompuy, such a supposed non-entity, was given chair of the European Council.

Next, cap spending on new IT schemes; it will be a big enough task getting the ones we have already to work properly. And we should do some proper counting up to see who lives in Britain. There has been a rag-bag of refugees and asylum seekers arriving. Nobody minds them being here. Polish shop assistants are often better educated and more charming than the English, and Afghan refugees often speak better English than British children, but we should know where, and who, these immigrants are. There has been so much slippage in the count. Can we have a one-off amnesty with protection for all? So many people have crept in and out of the country with our ever more relaxed borders, that amnesty must be the only way forward. Look at the debacle of the student visa system and the number of bogus colleges and bogus courses. It seemed that revenue, no matter where it came from and bugger the consequences, was the *sine qua non* of all that.

Thank goodness, and this *is* the bottom line, that England is a country that outsiders want to come to. There have been many waves of immigration. We remember drifts of Hungarian refugees, whose children turned up in our classrooms sometime during the fifties. We knew they were unfortunate and must be helped, which we did quietly and without fuss. Although we didn't have much ourselves back then, whatever we did have was shared. However, a word of caution. We are a welcoming, tolerant nation and have come a long way since words like illegitimate, cancer and divorce were purple, but newcomers should try to mind their p's & q's. They should show respect for British culture and not try to impose their own creeds upon us. Similarly, we should not be branded racist if we even dare stand against such things.

London is the hub of government activity but we wondered how much of this legislation and its supposed benefits filters out to Billericay, or down to Truro, or up to Carlisle? There are many quiescent people in the UK whose needs are never considered. They are like the quiet children at the back of the class who are no trouble, but lacking in confidence and often afraid to speak out. It is time the government gave these people a voice, in the same way that a good teacher would seek to draw students forward from the back of the class.

We hope the next prime minister doesn't take a look at health and education, find it too difficult, and resolve to make his name instead on the world stage, like so many PMs before him. We'd like to see a government looking about properly, not wasting time on the kind of meeting that Chris Mullin was sent to: a 'Listening to Old People' event. He describes it as 'a classic New Labour wheeze designed to create the illusion of consultation. A truly dire occasion.' What can this kind of thing actually be for other than job creation? It might be better if a few MPs and cabinet ministers drove about undercover, rather like the several months of travelling around Britain visiting local Conservative associations undertaken some years ago by Selwyn Lloyd and Ferdinand Mount.

We would like to see an end to the petty rivalries that go on between the parties, with one side often contradicting the other merely for the sake of it. Also they pinch each other's ideas and try to re-package them in the hope we do not notice. Why not just admit in the first place that there are subjects that could be agreed upon. There are too many sirens and buzzers sounding off. What the next government should do is to take stock and calm everyone down.

We (and very many others) have said this time and again, but what parents really want is just a good local school and a good local hospital, not lots of 'choices' outside the borough or across country. It sounds simple and it could be so. Although on this, governments are never 'on receive'. As Deborah Orr has written, and she is right, 'The worst schools are not compelled to improve because of parental choice they just end up populated by the children of the parents whose choices are fewest.' Affirmative action at university level doesn't mean you can bypass the greater difficulty of improving actual schools. Trying to push the middle classes out by pushing up the rest simply creates unfairness for another randomly chosen group. It is the teachers and nurses who suffer. The next government needs to find some better way of playing catch-up. If we are not careful we will have this not very bright boy removing your appendix and this clever boy, who also happened to go to a better school, taking away your rubbish. Success (and prosperity) comes from actual, not artificial achievement. Social mobility is in danger of being prioritised over meritocracy. Furthermore, if MPs can flip their homes, why not parents trying to get the best education for their child? One poor family was watched by undercover council officials after a tip off (unfounded as it turned out) that they were using a false address. Half a million parents submit appeals for school places and we bet a lot more people would too, if they thought it would get them anywhere.

And the next government needs to look at why we are at war in Afghanistan. And to what end? It beats us how a concept as vague as 'a war on terror' can be called a war in the first place, or that such a war can ever be won, unless you keep redefining what 'won' means and moving the parameters. And the goal posts have already been moved enough in both our recent conflicts. It is thought 100,000 people died in Iraq, very many of them not insurgents, but innocent victims.

As Anthony Sampson observed, there were connections between Suez and Iraq. This is what he said: 'Western Governments are enraged by a troublesome Arab dictator and decide to settle the score. But the political circumstances mean that they cannot openly avow what they are doing and so they embark on subterfuge and deception.'

And it is not over. In *Yo, Blair!*, Geoffrey Wheatcroft reports a leaked document from William Patey, the departing British ambassador in Baghdad: 'The prospect of a low intensity civil war and a de facto division of Iraq is probably more likely at this stage than a successful and substantial transition to a stable democracy.' Also, we still haven't found Osama and probably won't except by accident, rather like a lazy cat that finds a mouse running over its foot. It is not well known but according to *The Bumper Book of Government Waste*, defence chiefs spent £18,000 on a mystic powers experiment to find Bin Laden's lair.

Al-Qa'eda has moved its operation to the Yemen, and will probably move on from there. Which begs the question: are we in Afghanistan fighting the Taliban because women should be allowed to be educated and we want to help them, or because it is the hub of Islamic militancy, even though most terrorists were trained in Pakistan? For Afghan women we would say that education is the last thing they are worrying about right now. All they want is security and relief from the uncertainty and instability created by men. Different factions come and go leaving them no better off. If we are to do any good in Afghanistan we are in for the long haul and we doubt we are up to the task, although for the sake of their women we wish it were not so.

What governments should be doing is finding a way to solve the Arab-Israeli problem and helping the poor and dispossessed of Gaza. Bring back the road map. Tony Blair was wrong not to condemn the Israeli attack on Lebanon. He should have taken a leaf from Mrs Thatcher, who said, 'I do not believe in retaliatory strikes that are against international law.'

Until this problem is solved, nothing can be solved and no governments, particularly the British who marginalised Palestine in the first place, should think it can. It can't be impossible. As Anthony Sampson reports in his memoir, *The Anatomist,* ' "I love this dream," said Archbishop Desmond Tutu. "You sit in the balcony and look down and count all the terrorists. They are all sitting there passing laws. It is incredible." ' If this has come about in South Africa and Northern Island it can happen anywhere.

In spite of their many advisors, governments always seem to be bad at accountancy. The NHS Fraud Squad costs triple the amount of cash it delivers. Counter fraud cost £32.4 million, while it recovered £10.1 million. What a waste. Another example that comes immediately to mind is that during the pre-Christmas cold snap, minor roads weren't gritted and so our local A&E had 200 extra broken limbs because of it. Rolled across the country if you add up the cost to the NHS (factoring in many routine operations that had to be cancelled), how would this compare to the cost of grit? No joined-up thinking you see, councils wanting to keep to their budget couldn't care less about the cost to the NHS. What would it be to them? That 70s' phrase: 'Your problem.' It comes from having to be competitive not co-operative.

Old people are more vulnerable to falls, which brings us to the next demographic time-bomb. Sorry for the hyperbole, but if you don't call it a bomb of some kind nobody takes any notice. We are a nation of old people who are suddenly going to be very old and we need to be considered. There was a plaintive letter in a newspaper this week from a seventy-three-year-old man who had both parents still alive but no means of coping with himself and them financially, and in all probability in many other ways. This is why Mathew Taylor's idea of saving money (he is chief executive of a think tank, and a one time Downing Street Head of Policy) by providing state services mostly online is bananas.

It would provide yet more jobs for e-toolers, that's for sure, and certainly it would save money by disenfranchising all those old people, but it certainly wouldn't aid self-guided study. For NEETS? What could be more counter-productive? All it would do is reduce human contact for those who most need it. So not at all clever. And the idea that raising the birth rate and bringing more people into the country to raise funds is not the answer. We are too full as it is; more people would only compound the problem, or simply hand on the situation to the next generation.

We still haven't got our minds around global warming. Even if (a hugely unlikely if) climate change is not man-made, unless we take action our resources will run out. So whether it can be proved is an irrelevancy. It is a wake-up call for us to look at how we live. There are all sorts of small things we can do, which in time would amount to a lot and many are in our own interest. Eating less meat would help save the planet and lower our risk of cancer, for example. Many small changes to our lives are not difficult to do, but for them to make a difference, they require consensus and collective action. In the same way organically-farmed food may not be healthier necessarily, but it is certainly better for the countryside.

Cutting our birth rate can only be a good thing. In twenty years the UK population will be more than 70 million. This is too many people for a small island. If we save our primroses, celandines, bluebells, and woods, so much else is saved too. We must save the flowers *and* save the bees!

MPs should scrutinise their daily activities. Ask themselves is this a valid use of time or merely a vanity project and just a waste of trees? It was an ex-MP Anthony Cooms who in a letter to the *Telegraph* wrote: 'The age of instant communication and the Internet provide both excuse and alibi for valueless activity' – and we think he is right.

The next government should also remember that the point of politics is not just to acquire power and keep it. Power is not an end in itself. It is how you exercise it that counts. This was a description of the ninth Duke of Devonshire, who was appointed Governor General of Canada in 1916: 'there is a massive imper-turbability about him which gives confidence. He will never let one down, never play for his own advantage, never do anything brilliant . . . let us hope he will never do anything wrong.' This is the kind of Prime Minister we need right now.

Anthony Trollope was a particular admirer of Palmerston, whom he describes as bold, industrious, honest, strong in purpose and in health, eager and unselfish. Perhaps our next PM could think about how to acquire some of these qualities. We would add unflagging, defiant and courageous, especially the necessity of not doing anything brilliant in case it turned out to be calamitous. Could he focus on the good of the people instead of wasting time worrying about his legacy, or whether he will make a second term?

And if we could give the government one priority to work on, it is to lift the level of education of the country as a whole. As Keith Waterhouse said 'climb trees, play conkers, walk, think live', although get rid of those daft team-building exercises when everyone has to build a raft or trudge up a mountain and all the expected leaders 'lead' and lesser minions drag on behind just as they do back at the office. Without a better education we cannot expect the people to take responsibility for themselves. Nothing is as liberating as education.

We would like more than anything to see an electorate that is capable of calling the government to account. What we as a nation have become in the last few years is dull, pliable and standardised. We have been told our judgements are suspect, the most trivial decisions are questioned, and the most complex web of rules has taken even the smallest decision-making out of our hands. The more we are told we can't exercise judgement, the more it becomes self–fulfilling prophecy.

Who knows which party will get in next time, it could even be a hung parliament, but to quote one of the Kennedys, 'much is expected of those to whom much has been given'. This will be particularly important for the 'toffs' to remember if they are the victors. We would like opposing parties to find areas they can agree upon, take as much out of politics as possible and engage in much less squabbling. They must be big enough and brave enough to rise above the party and tell the truth as they see it (but not in the haltering 'I'm a pretty straight kind of guy' Blair-ish way). It was Albert Camus who said, 'If there were a party for those who weren't sure they were right I'd belong to it.'

And it would be better if there was a lot less bleating from on high. Natasha Engel has said, 'It's no fun being an MP and a mother.' Our answer would be don't do it then, wait till your children are a little older. Barack Obama was said to have been influenced by President Lincoln who appointed his one-time enemies to his cabinet and persuaded them to work for and with him. Even though she didn't bother to reply to our letter, if Caroline Lucas, leader of the Green Party, gets in for Brighton we think she should be given a cabinet seat. This is what Trollope's Prime Minister did to form a government. 'There were four or five certain names – names that is of certain political friends, and three or four almost equally certain of men *who had been political enemies* [our italics].' President Obama appointed Hillary Clinton as Secretary of State in much the same way.

And political parties should not take too much notice of the polls. We went to a lecture by Sir Robert Worcester, the opinion polster who founded MORI, during the lead up to the American elections. He said that Hillary Clinton would be made the Democrat candidate early in the race but the Republicans wouldn't settle on anyone for months. As it turned out the reverse was true. McCain was in straight away and Clinton and Obama fought to the last. It was Disraeli who said, 'There are three kinds of lies: Lies, damned lies and statistics.' Adam Smith was always very distrustful of statistics and according to his biographer, James Buchan, 'slept through the only lectures on political economy he is known to have attended'. He also said that 'a society does well to mingle with its politicians and poets, one or two weavers and ship-carpenters'. Something that should be considered when choosing candidates perhaps?

We would add that the study of history and philosophy should be mandatory for MPs, and not just a multiple-choice exam. Tony Blair, despite his Oxford education, showed astonishing ignorance of history when he waxed sentimental about the Americans standing side by side with us during the Blitz. In fact we desperately needed them and at that time they were nowhere to be seen. They didn't arrive at our side until after Pearl Harbor.

And Anthony Trollope has further advice, which is particularly useful given the frenzy of legislation during the past twenty years: 'A lengthened period of quiet and therefore good government would be the greatest benefit the country could ever receive.' As Seamus Heaney once said, 'Whatever you do, do nothing.'

The government should remind itself of its duty to hold the centre, steer away from excitable and keep the country strong and still. Remember 'solitude is the school for genius' and perhaps creativity is the 'still unravished bride of quietness'. Anthony Trollope's Prime Minister 'read the papers in solitude, because he was thus enabled to give his mind to their contents'. According to Ferdinand Mount, 'Mrs Thatcher did not appear to mind silence when she had nothing to say herself.' Neither was she much of a waffler. She gave Keith Joseph and Ferdinand Mount a telling off when they were trying to impress her:

'And what exactly would be the benefits of integrating these two branches of the service?' she said.

'Well, they would be, well, more co-ordinated.'

'That is surely another way of saying the same thing.'

Our dear 'right honourables' could forget about their obligation to entertain for a while, rather like 'don't bring Lulu, she'll come by herself' . . . There will always be more of Sally Bercow to look forward to.

What the electorate does not want to see in their politicians is just a mirror of our grasping, grabbing, acquisitive, image-driven selves. We would like someone to set an example. MPs should hold an ethical code in the back of their mind, like doctors who internalise their Hippocratic Oath, and they must not forget their humanity (or ours) in the struggle to 'make their mark'.

And we also need to set them a much better example. When everybody is fat, no one is. Norms are all relative. When everybody is cheating, no one is. 'It was within the rules'. Well, actually it wasn't.

And what do women want? What we are prepared to do is a lot of the cooking, cleaning and care, and much besides, but we don't want to do all of it and we would like what we do, usually unpaid, to be recognised and economically factored in. Theresa May said she was shocked how many people of working age were not economically productive. If she looks at unproductive women over fifty she might be surprised. For some reason, although women are frowned upon if they do not take on outside work, it is fine for older women to stay at home looking after the grandchildren. Cherie Blair, Caroline Flint and Yvette Cooper have all depended upon this kind of help. You can't visit a supermarket in the UK without seeing older women helping very much older women with their shopping. You have to be careful when you bandy about 'unproductive'. One thing we hope Theresa May gets rid of, if the Tories are in power, is HIPs (Home Information Packs) introduced by Yvette Cooper to supposedly make house buying easier and more 'transparent', which are hated by everyone and have had the opposite effect.

What women very definitely do not want are more sham consultations. As Richard Kersey, a village postmaster quoted in the *Telegraph*, said, 'The Government never had any intention of listening to our concerns. They wanted to close my post office and that was it.' We wouldn't mind betting that in time Adam Crozier (salary £1,038,000), who headed up the Post Office, will be discredited like Thomas Beeching.

And no more 'legally binding agreements' like guaranteeing everyone a tip top education, which are nothing but 'sound and fury, signifying nothing'. Nick Clegg's suggested 'Code of Conduct' for MPs sounds fine in principle, but how would it be policed? Whatever the legislation there will always be transgressors. Remember Alan Clark's diary and 'his glorious summer of 1955', when he was running Anne, Marye and Liz, all of them living within half a mile of each other, although we suppose nobody would bat an eyelid about that these days, unless the taxpayer was funding their rent.

There will always be human failure; top-secret documents will continue to be left on trains. Randolph Churchill once left classified military maps behind in Pamela's car. Pamela Harriman regarded mistakes as opportunities for growth, although we have no way of knowing whether Randolph thought the same. As Trollope says, 'wise men do foolish things at intervals. The discreetest of city bankers are talked out of their money; the most scrupulous of matrons are talked out of their virtue; the most experienced of statesmen are talked out of their principles.'

If Parliament was 'purified' would it be a better place? Blair promised that New Labour would be 'purer than pure'. Can this possibly be true? If so, he is an even bigger fool than we thought. There has not been the faintest whiff of scandal from Eric Pickles or Charles Clarke for example, but they are not the only character types we would like to see elected to the Commons.

It was Denis Thatcher who had the right idea about elections: 'Why we have to go through this carry-on for three bloody weeks is beyond me,' he said. 'After all, it's either, "Hello, it's me again," or, "Goodbye." '

At the next election there will be the biggest emptying out ('in out, in out, you do the hokey-cokey and you shake it all about', possibly half of the 646 MPs), a bigger influx of new faces than we have seen for years. We would like to see a fresh start, magnanimity in victory, whichever party it may be, and no energy misspent by settling old scores. Maybe electoral reform should be looked at again. Both major parties always promise this, until they get in and then it's a case of let's put that on the back burner.

And we hope women will have a voice. Recently it has been women who have 'made a difference' to so many important causes. For example, Joanna Lumley for the Gurkhas and Honor Blackman for Equitable Life. And it was Christine Lagarde, the French finance minister, who during the credit crunch spoke better sense than anyone, and what is more shocking still, in far better English than most of us did.

In her book about the sixties, Jenny Diski has reminded us all what we once thought: ideals should not be abandoned. 'We chose to believe (and I still like us for it) that everyone was capable of doing better – of having broader horizons, and of being educated into a wide curiosity that might mean they are dissatisfied with their lot, but which also gave them the tools for independent thought.'

We believe that everybody, particularly first-time voters, should go out and vote in the next election and at all elections afterwards. The silver lining of the credit crunch and the expenses scandal was the fact that it forced the electorate to sit up at last. We have to tub-thump on this point. And we know you can do it, since 10 million votes were cast on the last night of *The X Factor*!

And once you have voted keep a beady eye on those in power (bring on the whistle-blowers) and hold them to account at every twist and turn. Yes, make life difficult for them. As far as climate change is concerned, the young must band together and make the old sit up and take notice. Make those MPs stand up for principle and remember above all, as Edmund Burke said, 'All that is necessary for the triumph of evil is that good men do nothing.'

As Jenny Diski has said, 'It is not the job of the young to be grateful, it is their job to tear up the world and start again.'

Let us hope they do what we expect of them.

> Let us dream it now,
> And pray for a possible land
> Not of sleepwalkers, not of angry puppets,
> But where both heart and brain can understand
> The movements of our fellows;
> Where life is choice of instruments and none
> Is debarred his natural music,
> Where the waters of life are free of the ice-blockade of hunger
> And thought is free as the sun.

Louis MacNeice, *Autumn Journal*

Bibliography

Booker, Christopher & North, Richard: *Scared to Death*, Continuum 2007

Browne, Anthony: *The Retreat of Reason*, Civitas 2006

Buchan, James: *Adam Smith*, Profile 2007

Campbell, John: *If Love Were All*, Jonathan Cape 2006

Clark, Alan: *Diaries*, Phoenix 1993

Cope, Wendy: *If I Don't Know*, Faber & Faber 2001

Copperfield, David: *Wasting Police Time*, Monday Books 2006

Dale, Iain: *500 of the most Witty, Acerbic & Erudite things ever said about Politics*, Harriman House 2007

Diski, Jenny: *The Sixties*, Profile 2009

Donoughue, Bernard: *Downing Street Diary*, Pimlico 2006

Elliott, Matthew & Rotherham, Lee: *The Bumper Book of Government Waste*, Harriman House 2008

Goodwin, Doris Kearns: *Team of Rivals: The Political Genius of Abraham Lincoln*, Penguin 2009

Gray, Simon: *Coda*, Faber and Faber/Granta 2009

Hosken, Andrew: *Nothing Like A Dame: The Scandals of Shirley Porter*, Granta 2006

Larkin, Philip: *High Windows*, Faber and Faber, 1974

Leith, William: *Bits of Me Are Falling Apart*, Bloomsbury 2009

Letts, Quentin: *50 People Who Buggered Up Britain*, Constable and Robinson 2008

MacNeice, Louis: *The Collected Poems*, Faber & Faber 1966

Maitland, Sara: *A Book of Silence*, Granta 2009

McCarthy, Michael: *Say Goodbye to the Cuckoo*, John Murray 2009

McLoughlin, Jane: *A World According to Women*, Quartet 2009

Mount, Ferdinand: *Cold Cream: My Early Life and Other Mistakes*, Bloomsbury 2008

Mullin, Chris: *A View from the Foothills*, Profile 2009

Ogden, Christopher: *Pamela Harriman: Life of the Party*, Sphere 2006

Phillips, Adam: *Going Sane*, Penguin 2005

Rae, John: *The Old Boys' Network*, Short Books 2009

Robinson, Stephen: *The Remarkable Lives of Bill Deedes*, Abacus 2009

Sampson, Anthony: *The Anatomist*, Politico's 2008

Thatcher, Carol: *A Swim-on Part in the Goldfish Bowl*, Headline/Review 2009

Trollope, Anthony: *The Prime Minister*, Oxford University Press, Reissued 2008

Wheatcroft, Geoffrey: *Yo, Blair!*, Politico's 2007

Wheen, Francis: *Strange Days Indeed*, Fourth Estate 2009

Williams, Charles: *Harold Macmillan*, Weidenfeld & Nicolson 2009

Winnett, Robert & Rayner, Gordon: *No Expenses Spared*, Bantam 2009

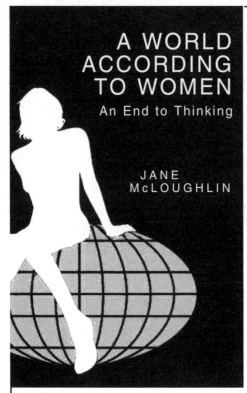

A WORLD ACCORDING TO WOMEN

An End to Thinking

JANE
McLOUGHLIN

This book will change the way you think . . . the most extraordinarily interesting and stimulating book, written with the passion of conviction.

FAY WELDON

Has feminism failed? Women have achieved lasting social change since the sixties, but it is not because of feminist politics.

McLoughlin's controversial premise is that modern feminism has failed 'ordinary women'. She argues that the feminist movement of the 1960s and 1970s only empowered the educated élite and uncommonly politicised. It was in fact popular culture – the emotionally driven and melodramatic world of day-time soap operas, paperback romance novels and vacuum-cleaner commercials – that has given economic power and political significance to the majority of women.

Women might have power now, says McLoughlin, but it is not a power based on reason, intelligence or hard work, but on the easily manipulated and negative nature of the popular culture which empowered them.

ISBN: 978 0 7043 7162 0   Paperback   202 pages   £10.00